Treasury of
Holiday
Recipes

PUBLICATIONS INTERNATIONAL, LTD.

Front cover photography by Photo/Kevin Smith, Chicago.

Pictured on the front cover *(clockwise from top left):* Regal Crown Roast of Pork
(page 48), Chocolate Whipped Cream Torte *(page 87),* Little Christmas Pizzas
(page 17), Almond Crescents *(page 63),* Christmas Tree Cookies *(page 63)* and
Chocolate Sugar Spritz *(page 69).*
Pictured on the back cover *(clockwise from top left):* Mini Sausage Quiches
(page 6), Cranberry Raisin Nut Bread *(page 34),* Gingerbread People *(page 74)* and
Fruited Pork Loin *(page 44).*

ISBN: 0-7853-2006-7

Manufactured in U.S.A.

8 7 6 5 4 3 2 1

Microwave Cooking: Microwave ovens vary in wattage. The microwave cooking
times given in this publication are approximate. Use the cooking times as guidelines
and check for doneness before adding more time. Consult manufacturer's instructions
for suitable microwave-safe cooking dishes.

Treasury of
Holiday
Recipes

Appetizers & Beverages

Mini Sausage Quiches

Makes 24 appetizers

- ½ **cup butter or margarine, softened**
- 3 **ounces cream cheese, softened**
- 1 **cup all-purpose flour**
- ½ **pound BOB EVANS FARMS® Italian Roll Sausage**
- 1 **cup (4 ounces) shredded Swiss cheese**
- 1 **tablespoon snipped fresh chives**
- 2 **eggs**
- 1 **cup half-and-half**
- ¼ **teaspoon salt**
- **Dash cayenne pepper**

Beat butter and cream cheese in medium bowl until creamy. Blend in flour; refrigerate 1 hour. Roll into 24 (1-inch) balls; press each into ungreased mini-muffin cup to form pastry shell. Preheat oven to 375°F. To prepare filling, crumble sausage into small skillet. Cook over medium heat until browned, stirring occasionally. Drain off any drippings. Sprinkle evenly into pastry shells in muffin cups; sprinkle with Swiss cheese and chives. Whisk eggs, half-and-half, salt and cayenne until blended; pour into pastry shells. Bake 20 to 30 minutes or until set. Remove from pans. Serve hot. Refrigerate leftovers.

Serving suggestion: Pour mixture into 12 standard 2½-inch muffin cups to make larger individual quiches. Serve for breakfast.

Miniature Seafood Cakes

Makes 24 appetizers

- ¼ cup reduced-calorie mayonnaise
- 1 egg, beaten
- 4 teaspoons lime juice
- ½ teaspoon grated lime peel
- ½ teaspoon hot pepper sauce
- 3 tablespoons finely chopped green onion
- 3 tablespoons finely chopped fresh parsley
- 1 pound crab-flavored surimi seafood, flakes, chunks or salad style, lightly chopped
- 2 cups fresh bread crumbs
  Nonstick cooking spray
  Low fat sour cream
  Caviar or paprika

Combine mayonnaise, egg, lime juice, lime peel and pepper sauce in medium bowl. Add green onion and parsley; mix well. Gently stir in surimi seafood and bread crumbs. Form mixture into 24 patties, each about 2 inches in diameter (mixture will be sticky).

Coat large nonstick skillet with cooking spray. Heat over medium-low heat until hot. Add 8 patties; cook 2 to 3 minutes per side or until brown. Remove to serving platter and keep warm while cooking remaining patties. Serve immediately. Top each patty with a dollop of sour cream and caviar.

*Favorite recipe from **National Fisheries Institute***

Holiday Seafood Spread

Makes 2½ cups spread or about 40 appetizer servings

- Nonstick cooking spray
- 1 carton (8 ounces) plain low fat yogurt
- ½ cup (4 ounces) light cream cheese, softened
- 1 tablespoon plus 1 teaspoon dried dill weed
- 1 teaspoon lemon juice
- ¼ teaspoon hot pepper sauce (optional)
- 12 ounces surimi seafood, crab or lobster flavored, flake or chunk style
  Butter lettuce leaves, for garnish
- 1 English cucumber, cut into ¼-inch-thick slices (about 40 slices)
  Assorted crackers

Line 1-quart bowl or mold with plastic wrap and coat with nonstick cooking spray. Combine yogurt, cream cheese, dill weed, lemon juice and hot pepper sauce, if desired, in food processor; process until smooth. Add surimi; process using on/off pulsing action until surimi is chopped. Spoon mixture into prepared bowl; cover and refrigerate 8 hours or overnight.

To serve, unmold onto lettuce-lined platter and remove plastic wrap. Serve with cucumber slices and crackers.

*Favorite recipe from **National Fisheries Institute***

Herbed Stuffed Mushrooms

Makes 24 appetizers

    24 large mushrooms
     2 teaspoons olive oil
     2 cloves garlic, minced
     1 package (10 ounces)
        frozen chopped spinach,
        thawed and well
        drained
     2 teaspoons dried basil
        leaves
     8 ounces crab-flavored
        surimi seafood, flakes,
        chunks or salad style,
        lightly chopped
     2 tablespoons grated
        Parmesan cheese

Preheat oven to 400°F. Remove stems from mushrooms; reserve for another use. Heat oil in large nonstick skillet over medium-high heat. Add garlic; cook 1 minute or until tender. Stir in spinach and basil; cook 1 minute. Stir in surimi seafood; remove from heat. Place mushrooms, rounded side down, on 15×10×1-inch jelly-roll pan. Spoon spinach mixture into caps; sprinkle with Parmesan cheese. Bake 8 to 10 minutes or until heated through. Serve immediately.

Favorite recipe from **National Fisheries Institute**

Clockwise from top left: Miniature Seafood Cakes, Herbed Stuffed Mushrooms and Holiday Seafood Spread

Baked Brie

Makes about 8 servings

> ½ **pound Brie cheese, rind removed**
> ¼ **cup chopped pecans**
> ¼ **cup KARO® Dark Corn Syrup**

Preheat oven to 350°F. Place cheese in shallow oven-safe serving dish. Top with pecans and corn syrup. Bake 8 to 10 minutes or until cheese is almost melted. Serve warm with plain crackers or melba.

Prep Time: 5 minutes
Bake Time: 8 minutes

Shrimp with Grapes and Mushrooms

Makes 4 servings

> 2 **teaspoons vegetable oil**
> 1 **pound medium to large shrimp, peeled and deveined**
> 8 **green onions, thinly sliced**
> 1 **tablespoon granulated sugar**
> ¼ **teaspoon black pepper**
> 1 **pound fresh mushrooms, sliced**
> 2 **tablespoons lemon juice**
> 2 **teaspoons Dijon mustard**
> 2 **cups halved grapes**

Heat oil in medium skillet. Add shrimp, green onions, sugar and pepper. Cook and stir about 5 minutes or until shrimp turn pink and opaque. Add mushrooms, lemon juice and mustard; cook and stir 2 minutes. Add grapes and cook about 2 minutes or until heated through. (Do not overcook.) Serve immediately.

Favorite recipe from ***The Sugar Association, Inc.***

Hot Spiced Cider

Makes about 10 (¾-cup) servings

> 2 **quarts apple cider**
> ⅔ **cup KARO® Light or Dark Corn Syrup**
> 3 **cinnamon sticks**
> ½ **teaspoon whole cloves**
> 1 **lemon, sliced**
> **Additional cinnamon sticks and lemon slices for garnish**

In 3-quart saucepan stir apple cider, corn syrup, cinnamon sticks, cloves and lemon slices. Bring to a boil. Reduce heat and simmer 15 minutes. Remove spices and lemon. Garnish each serving with a cinnamon stick and half a lemon slice.

Top to bottom: Hot Spiced Cider and Baked Brie

Party Cheese Wreath

Makes 2 cups

> 2 packages (8 ounces each)
> **PHILADELPHIA
> BRAND®** Cream Cheese,
> softened
> 1 package (8 ounces)
> **KRAFT®** Natural
> Shredded Sharp
> Cheddar Cheese
> 1 tablespoon *each* chopped
> red bell pepper and
> finely chopped onion
> 2 teaspoons Worcestershire
> sauce
> 1 teaspoon lemon juice
> Dash ground red pepper

• Beat cream cheese and Cheddar cheese with electric mixer at medium speed until well blended. Add bell pepper, onion, Worcestershire sauce, lemon juice and red pepper; mix well. Refrigerate several hours or overnight.

• Place drinking glass in center of serving platter. Drop rounded tablespoonfuls of mixture to form ring around glass, just touching outer edge of glass; smooth with spatula. Remove glass. Garnish with chopped fresh parsley and chopped red bell pepper. Serve with crackers.

May also use PHILADELPHIA BRAND® Neufchâtel Cheese, 1/3 Less Fat Than Cream Cheese or PHILADELPHIA BRAND FREE® Fat Free Cream Cheese.

Prep Time: 15 minutes plus refrigerating

Party Cheese Wreath

Mini Croquettes

Makes 25 to 30 appetizers

- **4 tablespoons butter or margarine, divided**
- **½ cup finely chopped fresh mushrooms (preferably cremini or shiitake)**
- **2 tablespoons minced green onion**
- **2 cups finely chopped cooked PERDUE® chicken or turkey**
- **¾ cup all-purpose flour, divided**
- **¾ cup chicken broth**
- **½ cup whipping cream**
- **2 teaspoons lemon juice**
- **⅛ teaspoon ground nutmeg Salt and black pepper**
- **1 egg, beaten**
- **½ cup seasoned bread crumbs Vegetable oil for deep frying**

Melt 1 tablespoon butter in large skillet over medium heat. Add mushrooms and green onion; cook and stir 5 minutes or until tender. Stir in chicken. Remove from heat; set aside. Combine remaining butter and 3 tablespoons flour in medium saucepan over medium heat. Cook 2 to 3 minutes until blended, stirring constantly and being careful not to brown. Gradually add broth; cook until smooth and thickened, stirring constantly. Stir in cream and lemon juice. Season with nutmeg, salt and pepper to taste. Add chicken mixture to cream sauce until combined; spread on large plate. Refrigerate 1 hour or until well chilled.

With measuring tablespoon, scoop out mixture; dip in remaining flour, egg and bread crumbs, coating all sides. Shape into small pyramids.

Heat 2 to 3 inches oil in large saucepan or deep fryer over medium-high heat until oil registers 375°F on deep-fat thermometer.

Fry croquettes a few at a time, being careful not to crowd, 30 seconds or until golden brown. Drain on paper towels. Serve warm.

Smucker's® Red Raspberry Mulled Cider

Makes 6 (6-ounce) servings

- **1 quart apple cider or apple juice**
- **½ cup SMUCKER'S® Seedless Red Raspberry Jam**
- **2 teaspoons lemon juice Cinnamon stick (optional)**

Combine cider and Smucker's® Seedless Red Raspberry Jam in nonaluminum saucepan. Whisk to dissolve jam; simmer until cider is warm. Add lemon juice. Pour into warm mugs. To serve, stir in cinnamon stick.

Note: Mulled cider may be prepared in advance and reheated in microwave oven in individual cups. Or, keep warm in decorative saucepan set over a chafing dish.

Chicken Saté

Makes 1⅓ cups sauce or about 3 dozen appetizers

> **Chicken Kabobs (recipe follows)**
> **1 teaspoon MAZOLA® Corn Oil**
> **1 teaspoon dark Oriental sesame oil**
> **¼ cup finely chopped onion**
> **1 clove garlic, minced**
> **½ teaspoon grated fresh ginger**
> **¼ teaspoon crushed red pepper (optional)**
> **½ cup SKIPPY® Creamy Peanut Butter**
> **¼ cup KARO® Light or Dark Corn Syrup**
> **1 tablespoon soy sauce**
> **1 tablespoon cider vinegar**
> **⅔ cup milk**

Begin preparing Chicken Kabobs. Meanwhile, in small saucepan heat oils over medium heat; add onion, garlic, ginger and crushed red pepper. Stirring constantly, cook 3 to 4 minutes or until onion is translucent. Stir in peanut butter, corn syrup, soy sauce and vinegar until smooth. Gradually stir in milk. Stirring constantly, bring to boil. Remove from heat. Cool slightly. Serve as dipping sauce for Chicken Kabobs.

Prep Time: 25 minutes, plus marinating
Broil Time: 6 minutes

Chicken Kabobs: Soak about 36 wooden skewers in water at least 20 minutes. In medium bowl combine 2 tablespoons Mazola® Corn Oil and 2 tablespoons light teriyaki sauce. Cut 1 pound boneless skinless chicken breasts into 1-inch pieces; stir into teriyaki mixture. Cover and let stand at room temperature no longer than 30 minutes or refrigerate several hours or overnight.

Thread chicken onto skewers. Place on foil-lined baking sheet. Broil about 6 inches from heat, 6 to 8 minutes or until lightly browned.

Hot Pineapple Port Cup

Makes 12 servings

> **6 cups DOLE® Pineapple Juice**
> **1 bottle (750 mL) port wine**
> **1 cup DOLE® Raisins**
> **½ cup sugar**
> **Peel of 1 Dole® Orange***

*Remove peel from orange with vegetable peeler.

Combine pineapple juice, wine, raisins, sugar and peel in Dutch oven. Heat to boiling. Remove from heat and steep 15 minutes.

Remove and discard peel before serving. Garnish with additional orange peel, if desired. Serve warm.

Top to bottom: Chicken Saté and Mustard-Glazed Shrimp (page 18)

14

PHILLY® Hot Crab Dip

PHILLY® Hot Crab Dip

Makes 10 to 12 servings

> 2 packages (8 ounces each) **PHILADELPHIA BRAND® Cream Cheese,** softened
>
> 2 cans (6 ounces each) **crabmeat, drained, flaked**
>
> ½ cup (2 ounces) **KRAFT® 100% Shredded Parmesan Cheese**
>
> ¼ cup **chopped green onions**
>
> 2 tablespoons **dry white wine (optional)**
>
> 2 teaspoons **KRAFT® Prepared Horseradish**
>
> ¼ teaspoon **hot pepper sauce**
>
> ⅓ cup **sliced almonds, toasted**

• Heat oven to 350°F.

• Mix all ingredients except almonds until well blended. Spoon into 9-inch pie plate or quiche dish; sprinkle with almonds.

• Bake 25 to 30 minutes or until lightly browned. Serve with assorted crackers.

May also use PHILADELPHIA BRAND® Neufchâtel Cheese, ⅓ Less Fat Than Cream Cheese or PHILADELPHIA BRAND FREE® Fat Free Cream Cheese.

Prep Time: 10 minutes
Cook Time: 30 minutes

Little Christmas Pizzas

Makes 40 appetizer servings

- 1/3 cup olive oil
- 3 tablespoons **TABASCO®** pepper sauce, divided
- 2 large cloves garlic, minced
- 1 teaspoon dried rosemary, crushed
- 1 (16-ounce) package hot roll mix with yeast packet
- 1 1/4 cups hot water

TOPPINGS

- 1 large tomato, diced
- 1/4 cup crumbled goat cheese
- 2 tablespoons chopped fresh parsley
- 1/2 cup shredded mozzarella cheese
- 1/2 cup pitted green olives
- 1/3 cup roasted red pepper strips
- 1/2 cup chopped artichoke hearts
- 1/2 cup cherry tomatoes, sliced into wedges
- 1/3 cup sliced green onions

In small bowl, combine olive oil, TABASCO sauce, garlic and rosemary. In large bowl, combine hot roll mix, yeast packet, hot water and 2 tablespoons TABASCO mixture; stir until dough pulls away from side of bowl. Turn dough onto lightly floured surface; shape dough into ball. Knead until smooth, adding additional flour as necessary.

Preheat oven to 425°F. Cut dough into quarters; cut each quarter into 10 equal pieces. Roll each piece into ball. On large cookie sheet, press each ball into 2-inch round. Brush each with remaining TABASCO mixture. Arrange approximately 2 teaspoons toppings on each dough round. Bake 12 minutes or until dough is lightly browned and puffed.

Stuffed Cheese Bread

Makes 16 servings

- 1 loaf (16 ounces) French bread, 24×4 inches
- 16 ounces Wisconsin Swiss cheese, shredded
- 1/2 cup butter, softened
- 1 can (4 ounces) mushroom stems and pieces, drained, chopped
- 2 tablespoons chopped onion
- 1 tablespoon prepared mustard
- 1 tablespoon poppy seeds
- 1 teaspoon seasoning salt
- 1/2 teaspoon lemon juice

Preheat oven to 350°F. Cut bread into 1 1/2-inch-thick slices, being careful not to cut through bottom of loaf. Cut loaf lengthwise across top perpendicular to slices, being careful not to cut through bottom. Combine cheese, butter, mushrooms, onion, mustard, poppy seeds, salt and lemon juice in large bowl; mix well. Spread cheese mixture onto slices. Wrap stuffed bread in aluminum foil and place on cookie sheet. Bake 30 to 40 minutes.

*Favorite recipe from **Wisconsin Milk Marketing Board***

17

Mustard-Glazed Shrimp

Makes 6 to 8 appetizer servings

MAZOLA No Stick® Corn Oil Cooking Spray
1 tablespoon dry mustard
2 tablespoons hot water
¼ cup **KARO® Light or Dark Corn Syrup**
¼ cup prepared duck or plum sauce
2 tablespoons rice wine or sake
1 tablespoon soy sauce
1 tablespoon dark Oriental sesame oil
1 pound large shrimp, shelled and deveined, or sea scallops
¾ pound sliced bacon, cut crosswise in half
Bamboo skewers, soaked in cold water 20 minutes

Line broiler pan rack with foil; spray with cooking spray. In small bowl stir mustard and water until smooth. Stir in corn syrup, duck sauce, rice wine, soy sauce and sesame oil. In large bowl toss shrimp with about ¼ cup of mustard glaze. Wrap half slice bacon around each shrimp and thread about 1 inch apart onto skewers.

Broil 6 inches from heat, 8 to 10 minutes or until shrimp are tender, turning and brushing occasionally with remaining mustard glaze.

Prep Time: 20 minutes
Broil Time: 10 minutes

Mushrooms Stuffed with Walnuts & Feta Cheese

Makes 4 appetizer servings

12 medium-size mushroom caps
1 tablespoon olive oil
1 tablespoon butter or margarine
½ cup finely chopped onion
2 tablespoons chopped walnuts
1 clove garlic, minced
5 ounces frozen chopped spinach, thawed and squeezed dry
1 ounce crumbled feta cheese
¼ cup (1 ounce) shredded Swiss cheese
2 tablespoons chopped fresh dill
Salt and black pepper to taste
Dry bread crumbs

Preheat oven to 400°F. Wipe mushroom caps with damp cloth; set aside. To prepare filling, heat oil and butter in large skillet over medium-high heat until hot; add onion. Cook, covered, until tender. Add walnuts and garlic. Cook and stir 1 minute. Stir in spinach, cheeses and dill. Remove from heat; blend well. Add salt and pepper. Stuff caps evenly with filling. Arrange caps, top sides down, in 8×8-inch baking dish. Sprinkle with bread crumbs. Bake 8 to 10 minutes or until browned. Serve warm. Refrigerate leftovers.

*Favorite recipe from **Bob Evans Farms**®*

Swiss Fondue-Wisconsin

Makes 6 servings

- **2 cups dry white wine**
- **1 tablespoon lemon juice**
- **1 pound Wisconsin Gruyère cheese, shredded**
- **1 pound Wisconsin Fontina cheese, shredded**
- **1 tablespoon arrowroot**
- **2 ounces kirsch**
  Pinch of ground nutmeg
  French bread cubes
  Pears, cut into wedges
  Apples, cut into wedges

Bring wine and lemon juice to a boil in fondue pot. Reduce heat to low. Toss cheeses with arrowroot. Gradually add to wine mixture, stirring constantly. When cheese is completely melted, stir in kirsch. Sprinkle with nutmeg and serve with French bread cubes, pears and apples.

*Favorite recipe from **Wisconsin Milk Marketing Board***

Salmon Appetizers

Makes 12 appetizers

- **1 package frozen puff pastry sheets**
- **4 ounces smoked salmon, flaked**
- **8 ounces cream cheese, softened**
- **2 tablespoons snipped chives**
- **1½ teaspoons lemon juice**

Preheat oven to 375°F. Cut 2-inch rounds of dough from pastry sheet; place in greased muffin cups. (Freeze remaining pastry sheet for later use.) Top dough rounds with salmon. Mix cream cheese, chives and lemon juice until creamy. Top salmon with about 1 tablespoon cream cheese mixture or pipe cream cheese over salmon, if desired. Bake 15 to 18 minutes. Serve warm.

*Favorite recipe from **Wisconsin Milk Marketing Board***

Left to right: Salmon Appetizers and Swiss Fondue-Wisconsin

Salads, Soups & Sides

Asparagus Wreath

Makes 4 side-dish servings

1 pound fresh asparagus, cleaned and steamed
1 tablespoon butter or margarine
1 teaspoon lemon juice
6 thin slices pepperoni, finely chopped
¼ cup seasoned dry bread crumbs
Pimiento strips for garnish

Arrange asparagus spears in glass ring mold or make wreath of spears on warm, round serving platter.

Melt butter and lemon juice in small saucepan over medium heat; pour over asparagus. Combine chopped pepperoni and bread crumbs in small bowl; sprinkle over asparagus. Garnish, if desired. Serve immediately.

Yorkshire Pudding

Makes 8 servings

>   2 eggs
>   1 cup all-purpose flour
>   ½ teaspoon salt
>   ¾ cup milk
>   ¼ cup water
>   1 package (1.0 ounce)
>   LAWRY'S® Seasoning
>   Blend for Au Jus Gravy
>   1½ cups water
>   ½ cup port wine
>   Dash LAWRY'S® Seasoned
>   Pepper
>   Vegetable oil

In medium bowl, using electric beater, beat eggs until frothy. Reduce speed and gradually add flour and salt; beat until smooth. Slowly add milk and ¼ cup water; beat until blended. Increase speed to high and continue beating 10 minutes. Let stand 1 hour. In medium saucepan, prepare Seasoning Blend for Au Jus Gravy with 1½ cups water, wine and Seasoned Pepper according to package directions. Set aside. Preheat oven to 400°F. Coat 5-inch omelette pan with oil and place in oven. When pan is very hot, remove and pour off excess oil. In pan, place 1 tablespoon Au Jus Gravy and ½ cup batter. Bake 20 to 30 minutes until puffed and brown. Remove and wrap in foil. Repeat until all batter has been used.

Presentation: Cut each pudding into quarters and serve with Prime Rib or Roast Beef. Serve remaining Au Jus Gravy over meat.

Hint: Pudding may be made ahead and reheated individually wrapped in foil.

Kielbasa & Chicken Gumbo

Makes 10 servings

>   6 slices bacon
>   1 pound BOB EVANS
>   FARMS® Kielbasa
>   Sausage, cut into 1-inch
>   pieces
>   ½ pound boneless skinless
>   chicken breasts, cut into
>   1-inch chunks
>   ¼ cup all-purpose flour
>   1 can (12 ounces) tomato
>   juice
>   1 cup water
>   1 can (28 ounces) whole
>   tomatoes, undrained
>   2 cubes chicken bouillon
>   1 can (8 ounces) tomato
>   sauce
>   1½ cups sliced fresh okra *or*
>   1 package (10 ounces)
>   frozen cut okra, thawed
>   1 medium onion, coarsely
>   chopped
>   1 medium green bell
>   pepper, coarsely
>   chopped
>   2 bay leaves
>   ½ teaspoon salt
>   ½ teaspoon ground red
>   pepper
>   ⅛ teaspoon ground allspice
>   1 pound uncooked medium
>   shrimp, peeled and
>   deveined
>   Hot cooked rice (optional)

Kielbasa & Chicken Gumbo

Cook bacon in large Dutch oven over medium-high heat until crisp. Remove bacon; drain and crumble on paper towel. Set aside. Cook and stir kielbasa and chicken in drippings over medium heat until chicken is lightly browned. Remove kielbasa and chicken; set aside. Drain off all but 3 tablespoons drippings from Dutch oven. Add flour to drippings; cook over medium heat 12 to 15 minutes or until a reddish-brown roux forms, stirring constantly. Gradually stir in tomato juice and water until smooth. Add tomatoes with juice and bouillon, stirring well to break up tomatoes. Add reserved kielbasa, chicken, tomato sauce, okra, onion, green pepper, bay leaves, salt, red pepper and allspice; mix well. Bring to a boil over high heat. Reduce heat to low; simmer, covered, 1 hour, stirring occasionally. Add shrimp and simmer, covered, 10 minutes more or until shrimp turn pink and opaque. Remove and discard bay leaves. Stir in reserved bacon. Serve hot over rice, if desired. Refrigerate leftovers.

Serving suggestion: Serve with cornbread.

23

Scallop and Yellow Rice Salad

Makes 5 servings

- ⅓ cup plus 2 tablespoons vegetable oil, divided
- ½ cup chopped onion
- 2 jalapeño or serrano peppers, seeded and minced*
- 1 clove garlic, minced
- 2 cups water
- ½ teaspoon ground turmeric
- ½ teaspoon ground cumin
- ½ teaspoon salt
- 1 cup uncooked long-grain white rice
- 1 pound bay scallops or quartered sea scallops
- 1 can (15 ounces) black beans, rinsed and drained
- 1 cup chopped tomatoes
- ¼ cup chopped fresh cilantro or parsley
- 3 tablespoons lime juice
  Lime wedges and zest for garnish

Jalapeño peppers can sting and irritate the skin; wear plastic disposable gloves when handling peppers and do not touch eyes. Wash hands after handling.

Heat 2 tablespoons oil in large saucepan over medium heat. Add onion, jalapeños and garlic. Cook and stir 3 to 4 minutes or until onion is softened. Add water, turmeric, cumin and salt. Bring mixture to a boil over high heat. Add rice; cover and reduce heat to low. Simmer 15 to 20 minutes or until most of the liquid is absorbed.

Stir in scallops; cover. Simmer 2 to 3 minutes or until scallops turn opaque and are cooked through. Transfer rice mixture to large bowl; set bowl in ice water. Toss mixture every few minutes. When mixture is lukewarm, stir in beans, tomatoes and cilantro.

Combine remaining ⅓ cup oil and lime juice in small bowl. Pour over salad and toss. Serve immediately or refrigerate. Garnish just before serving.

Tropical Holiday Salad

Makes 8 to 10 servings

- 2 cans (8 ounces each) DOLE® Pineapple Chunks in Juice, drained
- 1 package (8 ounces) DOLE® Pitted Dates
- 3 medium DOLE® Carrots, thinly sliced
- 2 DOLE® Oranges, peeled, sliced
- 2 DOLE® Bananas, peeled, sliced
- ¼ cup honey
- 2 tablespoons white wine vinegar
- 2 tablespoons lime juice
- 1 tablespoon vegetable oil
- 2 teaspoons grated lime peel

Combine all ingredients in large bowl.

Prep Time: 20 minutes

Scallop and Yellow Rice Salad

Scalloped Red Skin Potatoes

Makes 6 side-dish servings

4 tablespoons butter or margarine, divided
2 pounds red skin potatoes, cut into ¼-inch slices
2 tablespoons all-purpose flour
Salt, pepper and paprika
1¼ cups milk
Fresh thyme sprig for garnish

Preheat oven to 350°F. Grease 9-inch round baking dish with 1 tablespoon butter. Place potato slices on waxed paper and sprinkle with flour, tossing to coat. Place ⅓ of the potatoes in dish; sprinkle with salt, pepper and paprika to taste. Dot with 1 tablespoon butter. Repeat layers twice.

Heat milk in small saucepan over medium heat until hot *(do not boil)*. Pour over potatoes; sprinkle with salt, pepper and paprika. Cover with lid or aluminum foil. Bake 35 minutes. Uncover; bake 20 minutes more or until potatoes are fork-tender. Garnish, if desired. Serve immediately.

Scalloped Red Skin Potatoes

Smucker's® Waldorf Salad with Turkey and Apricot

Makes 6 servings

- ½ cup plain nonfat yogurt
- ⅓ cup SMUCKER'S® Apricot Preserves
- 1 tablespoon chopped dried tarragon, chives and parsley*
- 2 tablespoons lemon juice
- 1 teaspoon Dijon mustard
- ½ teaspoon lemon peel
- ½ teaspoon salt
- ⅛ teaspoon fresh ground black pepper
- 1 pound cooked boneless skinless turkey or chicken, cubed
- 1 red apple with skin, cut into ½-inch pieces
- 1 green apple with skin, cut into ½-inch pieces
- 2 ribs celery, cut into ¼-inch pieces
- ¼ cup raisins
- 6 lettuce leaves
- 1 tablespoon chopped fresh parsley or chives

1 teaspoon curry powder can be substituted for chopped herbs.

Combine yogurt, preserves, herbs, lemon juice, mustard, lemon peel, salt and pepper in large bowl; stir until well blended. Add turkey, apples, celery and raisins; stir to coat. Adjust seasoning to taste with additional salt and pepper.

Place lettuce leaf on each of 6 serving plates. Spoon salad on each plate. Garnish with parsley.

Glazed Acorn Squash

Makes 4 servings

- 2 medium acorn squash, halved and seeded
- 1½ cups cold tap water
- ⅓ cup KARO® Light or Dark Corn Syrup
- 1 tablespoon MAZOLA® Margarine or Butter, melted
- ½ teaspoon cinnamon
- ¼ teaspoon salt

Place squash cut-side down in 13×9×2-inch baking dish; add water. Bake in 400°F oven 30 minutes or until squash is fork-tender. Turn squash cut-side up. In small bowl combine corn syrup, margarine, cinnamon and salt. Spoon corn syrup mixture into squash cavities.

Bake in 350°F oven 15 minutes or until fork-tender, basting occasionally.

New England Clam Chowder

Makes 6 servings

- 24 medium clams, shucked
- 1 bottle (8 ounces) clam juice
- 3 medium potatoes, cut into ½-inch-thick slices
- ¼ teaspoon dried thyme leaves
- ¼ teaspoon ground white pepper
- 4 slices bacon, cut crosswise into ¼-inch strips
- 1 medium onion, chopped
- ⅓ cup all-purpose flour
- 2 cups milk
- 1 cup half-and-half
  Oyster crackers
  Fresh thyme for garnish

Coarsely chop clams with chef's knife; set aside.

Add bottled clam juice and enough water in glass measure to equal 2 cups; place in Dutch oven. Add potatoes, dried thyme and pepper; bring to a boil. Reduce heat; simmer 15 minutes or until potatoes are tender, stirring occasionally.

Cook bacon in medium skillet over medium heat until almost crisp. Add onion; cook until tender but not brown. Stir flour into bacon mixture. Whisk in milk using wire whisk. Cook until mixture boils and thickens. Add bacon mixture and half-and-half to potato mixture. Add clams and continue to heat until clams are firm. Serve with oyster crackers. Garnish, if desired.

Cinnamon Parsnip Soup

Makes 4 to 6 servings

- 2 tablespoons margarine or unsalted butter
- 1 medium onion, chopped
- 2 pounds parsnips, peeled and cut into 2-inch chunks
- 3 cups chicken broth
- ½ cup dry white wine
- ½ cup half-and-half
- ¼ teaspoon TABASCO® pepper sauce
  Ground cinnamon

• Combine margarine and onion in 3- to 4-quart saucepan. Cook over medium-high heat about 5 minutes, stirring often, until onion is translucent.

• Add parsnips and broth; bring to a boil over high heat. Reduce heat; cover and simmer about 30 minutes or until parsnips are very tender.

• Process mixture, a portion at a time, in food processor or blender until smooth. Return to saucepan. Stir in wine, half-and-half and TABASCO sauce; heat until steaming.

• Sprinkle individual servings with cinnamon.

New England Clam Chowder

Nutmeg & Honey Carrot Crescents

Makes 4 side-dish servings

- **1 pound fresh carrots, peeled**
- **⅓ cup water**
- **2 tablespoons honey**
- **¼ teaspoon grated fresh nutmeg**
- **2 tablespoons chopped walnuts**
- **2 edible flowers, such as snapdragons, for garnish**

To make carrot crescents, place 1 carrot on cutting board. Cut carrot in half lengthwise with utility knife. Place cut sides down. Hold carrot half flat to cutting board with one hand. Hold knife at a 45° angle, slanting it away from hand. Make ¼-inch-diagonal slices, beginning at large end of carrot. Repeat with remaining carrots.

Place carrot crescents and water in large saucepan; cover. Bring to a boil over high heat; reduce heat to medium-low. Simmer carrots about 8 minutes or until fork-tender. Transfer carrots to warm serving dish. Bring remaining liquid in saucepan to a boil until liquid is almost evaporated. Add honey and nutmeg; stir. Heat briefly and pour over carrots. Toss gently to coat. Sprinkle with walnuts. Garnish, if desired. Serve immediately.

Corn, Bacon & Rice Chowder

Makes 4 servings

- **1 package (7.2 ounces) RICE-A-RONI® Rice Pilaf**
- **2 tablespoons margarine or butter**
- **1 can (13¾ ounces) reduced-sodium or regular chicken broth**
- **1½ cups frozen corn *or* 1 can (16 or 17 ounces) whole kernel corn, drained**
- **1 cup milk**
- **1 cup water**
- **½ cup sliced green onions**
- **2 slices crisply cooked bacon, crumbled**

1. In 3-quart saucepan, sauté rice-pasta mix and margarine over medium heat, stirring frequently until pasta is lightly browned.

2. Stir in chicken broth and contents of seasoning packet; bring to a boil over high heat.

3. Cover; reduce heat. Simmer 8 minutes.

4. Stir in corn, milk, water and onions. Simmer, uncovered, 10 to 12 minutes, stirring occasionally. Stir in bacon before serving.

Potato & Cheddar Soup

Potato & Cheddar Soup

Makes 12 servings

- **2 cups water**
- **2 cups peeled and cubed red potatoes**
- **3 tablespoons butter or margarine**
- **1 small onion, finely chopped**
- **3 tablespoons all-purpose flour**
- **Ground red and black pepper to taste**
- **3 cups milk**
- **½ teaspoon sugar**
- **1 cup (4 ounces) shredded Cheddar cheese**
- **1 cup cubed cooked ham**

Bring water to a boil in large saucepan. Add potatoes and cook until tender. Drain, reserving liquid. Measure 1 cup liquid, adding water if necessary. Melt butter in saucepan over medium heat. Add onion; cook and stir until tender but not brown. Add flour; season with red and black pepper. Cook 3 to 4 minutes. Gradually add potatoes, reserved liquid, milk and sugar to onion mixture; stir well. Add cheese and ham. Simmer over low heat 30 minutes, stirring frequently.

Green Beans with Basil Orange Cream

Makes 4 side-dish servings

> 1 pound fresh green beans
>   Salt and black pepper to taste
> 2 tablespoons mayonnaise or salad dressing
> 2 tablespoons plain low fat yogurt
> ½ cup whipping cream
> 2 teaspoons snipped fresh basil *or* ½ teaspoon dried basil leaves
> 1 teaspoon water
> ½ teaspoon grated orange peel
>   Halved orange slices (optional)
>   Fresh basil sprigs (optional)

Steam beans in 2-quart saucepan until crisp-tender; drain. (Do not overcook.) Transfer beans to platter; sprinkle lightly with salt and pepper. Cover and keep warm. Combine mayonnaise and yogurt in small bowl; set aside. Combine cream, snipped basil, water and orange peel in small nonaluminum saucepan. Cook, uncovered, over medium-low heat until thickened, stirring occasionally with rubber spatula. Whisk cream mixture into mayonnaise mixture until smooth. Garnish beans with orange slices and basil sprigs, if desired. Serve beans hot with orange cream mixture. Refrigerate leftovers.

*Favorite recipe from **Bob Evans Farms**®*

Creamed Pearl Onions

Makes 4 side-dish servings

> 1 pint pearl onions (about 10 ounces), peeled
> 2 tablespoons butter or margarine
> 2 tablespoons all-purpose flour
> 1 cup half-and-half
> ¼ teaspoon *each* salt and pepper
> ¼ cup dry bread crumbs
>   Red onion slices and fresh sage leaves for garnish

Place onions in 2-quart saucepan with ½ inch of water; cover. Bring to a boil over high heat; reduce heat to medium-low. Simmer 15 to 20 minutes or until fork-tender. Drain; set aside.

To make cream sauce, melt butter in small saucepan over medium heat. Blend in flour with wire whisk. Heat until mixture bubbles. Whisk in half-and-half. Cook until mixture thickens, whisking constantly. Add salt and pepper. Stir in cooked onions. Transfer creamed onions to warm serving bowl. Sprinkle with dry bread crumbs. Garnish, if desired. Serve immediately.

Breads & Coffee Cakes

Cranberry Raisin Nut Bread

Makes one 8¹/₂×4¹/₂-inch loaf

- 1½ cups all-purpose flour
- ¾ cup packed light brown sugar
- 1½ teaspoons baking powder
- ½ teaspoon *each* baking soda, ground cinnamon and ground nutmeg
- 1 cup halved fresh or frozen cranberries
- ½ cup *each* golden raisins and coarsely chopped pecans
- 1 tablespoon grated orange peel
- 2 eggs
- ¾ cup milk
- 3 tablespoons butter or margarine, melted
- 1 teaspoon vanilla

Preheat oven to 350°F. Grease 8½×4½-inch loaf pan. Combine flour, brown sugar, baking powder, baking soda, cinnamon and nutmeg in large bowl. Stir in cranberries, raisins, pecans and orange peel. Mix eggs, milk, butter and vanilla in small bowl until combined; stir into flour mixture just until moistened. Spoon into prepared pan.

Bake 55 to 60 minutes or until wooden pick inserted in center comes out clean. Cool in pan 15 minutes. Remove from pan and cool completely on wire rack. Store tightly wrapped in plastic wrap at room temperature.

Norwegian Almond Muffins

Norwegian Almond Muffins

Makes 12 muffins

2 cups all-purpose flour, divided
1 package RED STAR® Active Dry Yeast or QUICK•RISE™ Yeast
¼ cup sugar
1 teaspoon salt
1 teaspoon ground cardamom
½ cup water
¼ cup milk
¼ cup butter or margarine
¼ cup almond paste
1 egg
½ teaspoon almond extract
⅛ cup cherry preserves
1 tablespoon sugar
¼ cup chopped almonds

Preheat oven to 350°F.

Combine 1 cup flour, yeast, ¼ cup sugar, salt and cardamom in small bowl; mix well. Heat water, milk, butter and almond paste until very warm (120° to 130°F; butter does not need to melt). Add to flour mixture. Add egg and almond extract. Beat with electric mixer at low speed until moistened. Beat 3 minutes at medium speed. By hand, gradually stir in remaining 1 cup flour to make soft batter.

Spoon batter into well-greased muffin cups. Cover; let rise in warm place 1 to 1½ hours (30 to 45 minutes for QUICK•RISE™ Yeast).

Before baking, make an indentation in top of each muffin; spoon about ½ teaspoon cherry preserves into each muffin. Combine 1 tablespoon sugar and almonds; sprinkle over muffins. Bake 20 to 25 minutes or until golden brown. Cool in pans 3 minutes; remove from pans. Serve warm or cold.

Cheesy Date Nut Loaf

Makes 1 loaf

> ¾ cup boiling water
> ½ pound finely chopped dates (1⅛ cups)
> 2 tablespoons butter
> 1¾ cups all-purpose flour
> ½ cup sugar
> 1 teaspoon baking soda
> ¼ teaspoon salt
> 1 egg, beaten
> 1 cup (4 ounces) shredded Wisconsin Cheddar cheese
> 1 cup chopped walnuts

Preheat oven to 325°F. Pour boiling water over dates and butter. Let stand 5 minutes. Sift together dry ingredients. Add cooled date mixture, egg, cheese and nuts. Mix just until dry ingredients are moistened.

Pour mixture into well-buttered 9×5×3-inch loaf pan. Let stand 20 minutes. Bake 50 to 60 minutes or until wooden pick inserted in center comes out clean. Turn out onto wire rack to cool.

*Favorite recipe from **Wisconsin Milk Marketing Board***

Pineapple Orange Walnut Bread

Makes 12 servings

> 2 cups all-purpose flour
> 1 teaspoon baking powder
> ½ teaspoon baking soda
> ¼ teaspoon salt
> ¼ cup margarine
> ¾ cup sugar
> 1 egg
> ¼ cup orange juice
> 1 tablespoon grated orange peel
> 1 can (8 ounces) DOLE® Crushed Pineapple in Juice, undrained
> 1 cup DOLE® Seedless or Golden Raisins
> 1 cup chopped walnuts, toasted

• Combine flour, baking powder, baking soda and salt in medium bowl; set aside.

• Beat together margarine and sugar in large bowl until light and fluffy. Beat in egg, orange juice and orange peel. Alternately stir in one-third flour mixture and one-half undrained pineapple until just blended, ending with flour. Stir in raisins and walnuts.

• Pour batter into 9×5-inch loaf pan coated with nonstick cooking spray.

• Bake at 350°F 60 to 70 minutes or until toothpick inserted in center comes out clean. Cool in pan 10 minutes; remove from pan and cool completely on wire rack.

Prep Time: 20 minutes
Bake Time: 70 minutes

Fruited Oat Scones

Makes 1 dozen scones

1½ cups all-purpose flour
1¼ cups QUAKER® Oats
   (quick or old fashioned,
   uncooked)
¼ cup sugar
1 tablespoon baking
   powder
¼ teaspoon salt (optional)
⅓ cup (5⅓ tablespoons)
   margarine
1 (6-ounce) package
   (1⅓ cups) diced dried
   mixed fruit
½ cup milk
1 egg, slightly beaten
1 teaspoon sugar
⅛ teaspoon ground
   cinnamon

Preheat oven to 375°F. Combine flour, oats, ¼ cup sugar, baking powder and salt; mix well. Cut in margarine until mixture resembles coarse crumbs; stir in fruit. Add milk and egg, mixing just until moistened. Shape dough to form a ball. Turn out onto floured surface; knead gently 6 times. On lightly greased cookie sheet, pat out dough to form 8-inch circle. With sharp knife, score round into 12 wedges; sprinkle with combined 1 teaspoon sugar and cinnamon. Bake about 30 minutes or until golden brown. Break apart; serve warm.

Date Citrus Muffins

Makes 12 muffins

⅓ cup honey
¼ cup margarine, softened
1 egg
1 can (8 ounces) DOLE®
   Crushed Pineapple in
   Juice, undrained
1 tablespoon grated orange
   peel
1 cup all-purpose flour
1 cup whole wheat flour
1½ teaspoons baking powder
¼ teaspoon salt
¼ teaspoon ground nutmeg
1 cup DOLE® Chopped
   Dates
½ cup DOLE® Chopped
   Almonds, toasted

• Beat honey and margarine 1 minute in large bowl. Beat in egg, crushed pineapple and orange peel.

• Combine remaining ingredients. Stir into pineapple mixture until just blended.

• Spoon batter into greased muffin pans. Bake at 375°F 25 minutes. Turn out onto rack to cool.

Prep Time: 10 minutes
Bake Time: 25 minutes

Fruited Oat Scones

Spicy Buns

Makes 24 to 30 buns

**3½ to 4 cups all-purpose
    flour, divided
2 packages RED STAR®
    Active Dry Yeast or
    QUICK•RISE™ Yeast
⅓ cup sugar
1 teaspoon salt
½ teaspoon ground
    cinnamon
½ teaspoon ground nutmeg
¼ teaspoon ground mace
⅛ teaspoon ground ginger
⅔ cup water
½ cup butter or margarine
3 eggs
1 cup raisins or currants**

Preheat oven to 350°F.

Combine 2 cups flour, yeast, sugar, salt, cinnamon, nutmeg, mace and ginger in large bowl; mix well. Heat water and butter until very warm (120° to 130°F; butter does not need to melt). Add to flour mixture. Add eggs. Blend with electric mixer at low speed until moistened. Beat 3 minutes at medium speed. By hand, stir in raisins and enough remaining flour to make firm dough. Knead dough on floured surface until smooth and elastic, about 5 minutes. Place dough in greased bowl, turning to grease top. Cover; let rise in warm place until light and doubled in bulk, about 1 hour (30 minutes for QUICK•RISE™ Yeast).

Spicy Buns

Punch down dough. On lightly floured surface, roll dough to ½-inch thickness. Cut out buns with 1½ to 2-inch round cutter. Place on greased cookie sheets, 1½ inches apart. Cover; let rise in warm place until light and doubled in bulk, about 30 minutes (15 minutes for QUICK•RISE™ Yeast). Bake 10 to 12 minutes or until golden brown. Cool on racks. Drizzle with powdered sugar icing, if desired. Best served warm.

Wild Rice Three Grain Bread

Makes 1 braided wreath or 2 pan loaves

>   1 package active dry yeast
>   ⅓ cup warm water (105° to 115°F)
>   2 cups milk, scalded, cooled (105° to 115°F)
>   2 tablespoons shortening, melted
>   ½ cup honey
>   2 teaspoons salt
>   4 to 4½ cups bread flour, divided
>   2 cups whole wheat flour
>   ½ cup rye flour
>   ½ cup uncooked rolled oats
>   1 cup cooked wild rice
>   1 egg, beaten with 1 tablespoon water
>   ½ cup hulled sunflower seeds (optional)

Sprinkle yeast over water in large bowl; stir until yeast is dissolved. Add milk, shortening, honey and salt. Stir in 2 cups bread flour, whole wheat flour, rye flour and oats to make soft dough. Add wild rice. Cover and let rest 15 minutes. Stir in enough additional bread flour to make stiff dough. Turn out dough onto bread board; knead 10 minutes. Add more flour if necessary to prevent dough from sticking. Place dough in lightly greased bowl; turn dough over so that top is greased. Cover; let rise until doubled, about 2 hours. Punch down dough. Knead briefly on lightly oiled board. Divide dough into thirds and shape into strands. Braid strands and place onto greased baking sheet and form a wreath. Or, divide dough into 2 parts and place into 9½×5½-inch greased loaf pans. Let rise until doubled in bulk, about 45 minutes. Brush tops of loaves with egg. Slash loaves and sprinkle with sunflower seeds, if desired. Bake at 375°F 45 minutes or until loaves sound hollow when tapped.

*Favorite recipe from **Minnesota Cultivated Wild Rice Council***

Tomato-Artichoke Focaccia

Makes 16 servings

> **1 package (16 ounces) hot roll mix**
> **2 tablespoons wheat bran**
> **1¼ cups hot water**
> **4 teaspoons olive oil, divided**
> **1 cup thinly sliced onions**
> **2 cloves garlic, minced**
> **1 cup rehydrated sun-dried tomatoes (4 ounces dry), cut into strips**
> **1 cup artichoke hearts, sliced**
> **1 tablespoon minced fresh rosemary**
> **2 tablespoons freshly grated Parmesan cheese**

Preheat oven to 400°F. Combine dry ingredients and yeast packet from hot roll mix in large bowl. Add bran; mix well. Stir in hot water and 2 teaspoons oil. Knead dough about 5 minutes or until ingredients are blended.

Spray 15½×11½-inch baking pan *or* 14-inch pizza pan with nonstick cooking spray. Press dough onto bottom of prepared pan. Cover; let rise 15 minutes.

Heat 1 teaspoon oil in medium skillet over low heat. Add onions and garlic; cook and stir 2 to 3 minutes or until onions are tender.

Tomato-Artichoke Focaccia

Brush surface of dough with remaining 1 teaspoon oil. Top dough with onion mixture, tomatoes, artichokes and rosemary. Sprinkle with Parmesan. Bake 25 to 30 minutes or until lightly browned on top. Cut into squares. Garnish each square with fresh rosemary sprigs, if desired.

Tropical Banana Bread

Makes 18 servings

> 2 cups all-purpose flour
> 2 teaspoons baking powder
> ½ teaspoon salt
> ½ teaspoon ground ginger
> ½ cup margarine, softened
> 1 cup sugar
> 2 eggs
> 2 ripe medium DOLE® Bananas, mashed (about ¾ cup)
> 2 teaspoons grated orange peel
> ½ cup finely chopped dried papaya
> ½ cup chopped macadamia nuts, toasted
> ¼ cup flaked coconut, toasted
> Orange Icing (recipe follows)

• Combine flour, baking powder, salt and ginger in medium bowl; set aside.

• Beat together margarine and sugar in large bowl until creamy. Beat in eggs, bananas and orange peel until blended. Stir in flour mixture, papaya, nuts and coconut until combined. Spoon evenly into 3 mini loaf pans (5¾×3½-inch) coated with nonstick cooking spray.*

• Bake at 350°F 45 to 50 minutes or until toothpick inserted in center comes out clean. If bread begins to get too brown, cover loosely with foil. Cool in pans 15 minutes. Remove from pans and cool completely on wire rack. Drizzle with icing.

Orange Icing: Combine 1 cup powdered sugar with 1 to 2 tablespoons orange juice; stir until smooth.

Prep Time: 20 minutes
Bake Time: 50 minutes

*For larger loaf: Spoon prepared batter into 9×5-inch bread pan. Bake at 350°F 60 to 70 minutes or until toothpick comes out clean. Cool and drizzle with icing as directed above.

Entrées

Fruited Pork Loin

Makes 6 to 10 servings

1 cup dried apricot halves
½ cup dry sherry
1 (3- to 5-pound) center cut pork rib or loin roast, backbone cracked
1 cup KARO® Light or Dark Corn Syrup
1 tablespoon grated orange peel
½ cup orange juice
¼ cup soy sauce

In small saucepan, combine apricots and sherry. Cover and cook over medium heat, stirring occasionally, until liquid is absorbed. Trim excess fat from surface of roast. Cut deep slits in meat directly over rib bones; insert 3 or 4 apricots in each slit. Place roast, bone-side down, on rack in roasting pan.

Roast in 325°F oven 1 to 2 hours* or until meat thermometer registers 160°F. Meanwhile, prepare glaze. In small saucepan, stir corn syrup, orange peel, orange juice and soy sauce. Bring to boil; reduce heat and simmer 5 minutes. Set aside half of glaze to serve with pork loin. Brush pork loin frequently with remaining glaze during last 30 minutes of roasting. Serve with reserved glaze.

Prep Time: 20 minutes
Bake Time: 1 to 2 hours

Roast pork loin at 325°F for 20 to 25 minutes per pound.

Fruited Pork Loin with Glazed Acorn Squash (page 27)

Beef Tenderloin Dijon

Makes 8 servings

**1 beef tenderloin roast
(about 2 pounds)
1½ teaspoons salt, divided
¾ teaspoon black pepper,
divided
2 tablespoons olive oil
2 cloves garlic, minced
4 cups water
2 cans (10¾ ounces each)
condensed beef broth
1 bay leaf
½ teaspoon dried thyme
leaves
2 whole cloves
1 tablespoon *each*
cornstarch and Dijon
mustard**

Tie beef tenderloin roast with heavy string at 2-inch intervals. Combine 1 teaspoon salt and ½ teaspoon pepper; rub on surface of roast. Heat oil in Dutch oven over medium-high heat. Add roast and garlic; cook about 6 minutes or until evenly browned. Remove roast from pan; pour off drippings. Add water, broth, bay leaf, thyme and cloves to pan; bring to a boil. Add roast; reduce heat to medium-low. Cover and simmer about 20 minutes. Check temperature with instant-read thermometer; temperature should register 130°F for rare. *Do not overcook.* Remove roast to serving platter. Cover tightly with plastic wrap or foil and allow to stand 10 minutes before carving. (Roast will continue to rise about 10°F in temperature to 140°F for rare.)

Strain cooking liquid; reserve 2 cups. Remove Dutch oven from heat; add cornstarch and mustard, mixing to form a thick paste. Gradually add reserved cooking liquid, stirring constantly. Place Dutch oven over medium heat; add remaining ½ teaspoon salt and ¼ teaspoon pepper. Cook about 7 minutes or until slightly thickened. Remove strings from roast. Carve into thin slices. Serve roast with sauce and steamed vegetables, if desired.

Note: A beef tenderloin roast will yield four 3-ounce cooked servings per pound.

*Favorite recipe from **National Cattlemen's Beef Association***

Prime Rib of Beef à la Lawry's®

Makes 8 servings

**1 (8-pound) prime rib roast
LAWRY'S® Seasoned Salt
Rock salt**

Preheat oven to 500°F. Score fat on meat and rub generously with Seasoned Salt. Cover bottom of roasting pan with rock salt 1 inch thick. Place roast directly on rock salt and roast, uncovered, 8 minutes per pound for rare.

Presentation: Garnish with watercress and spiced crab apples. Carve at tableside.

Beef Tenderloin Dijon

Regal Crown Roast of Pork

Makes 8 servings

- 1 (16 rib) pork crown roast
  Salt and pepper
- 2/3 cup sliced leek
- 1/2 cup sliced celery
- 4 tablespoons butter or margarine
- 1 large apple, cored and diced
- 12 Thick-style KAVLI® Crispbreads
- 1 cup finely diced JARLSBERG Cheese
- 1/2 cup dried cherries or dried cranberries
- 1/4 cup chopped parsley
- 2 teaspoons salt
- 1/2 teaspoon ground pepper
- 1/2 cup white wine or unsweetened apple juice
  Pan Sauce (recipe follows)
  Steamed baby carrots and leek bundles (optional)

Preheat oven to 325°F. Rub roast with salt and pepper. Place in shallow roasting pan; insert meat thermometer into thickest part of roast not touching bone. Roast 1 hour and 45 minutes or until thermometer registers 150°F.

While roast cooks, prepare stuffing. Cook leek and celery in butter 5 minutes; stir in apple and cook 3 minutes longer. Remove from heat. Crush or cut crispbreads into 1/2-inch pieces (about 2 cups). Place in large bowl; add cheese, cherries, parsley, salt, pepper and apple mixture; mix well. Sprinkle with wine; toss until evenly moistened.

Remove roast from oven. Spoon stuffing into center, mounding it. (Spoon any extra stuffing into small buttered casserole to bake along with roast.) Return roast to oven and roast about 1 hour or until thermometer registers 160°F or slightly lower. (Meat will continue to cook as it stands.) Remove roast to serving platter and keep warm. Let rest at least 10 minutes. Prepare Pan Sauce. To serve, carve between ribs. Decorate platter with steamed baby carrots and bundles of small leeks. Serve with Pan Sauce.

Pan Sauce: Deglaze roasting pan with 1 cup water and 1/2 cup white wine; strain into small saucepan. Skim off fat. Bring to a boil. Blend 2 tablespoons flour with 3 to 4 tablespoons cold water to make smooth paste. Add to boiling liquid, stirring constantly, until thickened. Lower heat and simmer on low 5 minutes. Add salt and pepper to taste.

Grilled Swordfish à l'Orange

Grilled Swordfish à l'Orange

Makes 4 servings

**4 swordfish, halibut or
    shark steaks (about
    1½ pounds)**
¾ cup orange juice
1 tablespoon lemon juice
1 tablespoon sesame oil
1 tablespoon soy sauce
**1 teaspoon orange peel,
    divided**
**1 teaspoon cornstarch
    Salt and black pepper to
    taste**
1 orange, sectioned

Rinse swordfish and pat dry with paper towels.

Combine orange juice, lemon juice, oil and soy sauce in small bowl. Pour half of orange juice mixture into shallow glass dish. Add ½ teaspoon grated orange peel to orange juice mixture. Coat fish in mixture; cover and allow to marinate in refrigerator for at least 1 hour.

Place remaining half of orange juice mixture in small saucepan. Stir in cornstarch and remaining ½ teaspoon orange peel. Heat over medium-high heat, stirring constantly, 3 to 5 minutes or until sauce thickens; set aside.

Remove fish from marinade; discard remaining marinade. Lightly sprinkle fish with salt and pepper to taste. Grill 3 to 4 minutes per side or until fish is opaque and flakes easily when tested with fork. Top with orange sections and orange sauce. Serve immediately.

Cheese Tortellini with Tuna

Makes about 4 (1½-cup) servings

- **1 tuna steak (about 6 ounces)**
  Nonstick cooking spray
- **1 cup finely chopped red bell pepper**
- **1 cup finely chopped green bell pepper**
- **¼ cup finely chopped onion**
- **¾ teaspoon fennel seeds, crushed**
- **½ cup evaporated skim milk**
- **2 teaspoons all-purpose flour**
- **½ teaspoon dry mustard**
- **½ teaspoon black pepper**
- **1 package (9 ounces) cheese tortellini, cooked and drained**

Grill or broil tuna, 4 inches from heat source, 7 to 9 minutes or until fish just begins to flake. Remove and discard skin. Cut tuna into chunks; set aside.

Spray large nonstick skillet with cooking spray. Add bell peppers, onion and fennel seeds; cook over medium heat until crisp-tender.

Whisk together milk, flour, mustard and black pepper in small bowl until smooth; add to skillet. Cook until thickened, stirring constantly. Stir in tuna and pasta; reduce heat and simmer about 3 minutes or until heated through. Serve immediately.

Roast Pork with Banana Sauce

Makes 6 servings

- **1 pork loin roast (about 3 pounds)**
- **1 tablespoon vegetable oil**
  LAWRY'S® Seasoned Salt to taste
  LAWRY'S® Seasoned Pepper to taste
- **¼ cup LAWRY'S® Minced Onion with Green Onion Flakes**
- **¼ teaspoon LAWRY'S® Garlic Powder with Parsley**
- **1 can (4 ounces) diced green chilies**
- **2 ripe bananas**
- **1½ cups orange juice**

Preheat oven to 350°F. In large skillet, brown pork on all sides in hot oil; remove from pan. Season pork with Seasoned Salt, Seasoned Pepper, Minced Onion with Green Onion Flakes and Garlic Powder with Parsley. Place in roasting pan. Purée remaining ingredients in food processor, using steel blade. Pour sauce over roast; cover and cook 1½ to 2 hours, basting frequently. Remove roast to serving platter; keep warm. Skim fat from sauce. Serve sauce in separate bowl.

Presentation: Serve with cooked rice or buttered egg noodles.

Cheese Tortellini with Tuna

Spinach-Stuffed Chicken Breasts

Makes 4 servings

- **2 boneless skinless chicken breasts (8 ounces each), halved**
- **5 ounces frozen chopped spinach, thawed, well drained**
- **2 tablespoons freshly grated Parmesan cheese**
- **1 teaspoon grated lemon peel**
- **¼ teaspoon black pepper Nonstick cooking spray**
- **1 cup thinly sliced mushrooms**
- **6 slices (2 ounces) thinly sliced low fat turkey-ham**
- **1 cup Catawba juice***

*Or, substitute white grape juice.

Preheat oven to 350°F. Pound chicken breasts to ¼-inch thickness with flat side of meat mallet or chef's knife. Combine spinach, Parmesan, lemon peel and pepper in large bowl.

Spray small nonstick skillet with cooking spray; add mushrooms. Cook and stir over medium heat 3 to 4 minutes or until tender. Arrange 1½ slices turkey-ham over each chicken breast half. Spread each with ¼ of the spinach mixture. Top each with mushrooms. Beginning with longer side, roll chicken tightly. Tie with kitchen string.

Place stuffed chicken breasts in 9-inch square baking pan, seam side down. Lightly spray chicken with cooking spray. Pour Catawba juice over top. Bake 30 minutes or until chicken is no longer pink. Remove string; cut chicken rolls into ½-inch-diagonal slices. Arrange on plate. Pour pan juices over chicken. Garnish as desired.

Old Country Quiche

Makes 6 servings

- **½ cup chopped onion**
- **2 tablespoons butter**
- **6 slices cooked bacon, crumbled**
- **2 cups (8 ounces) shredded Wisconsin Swiss cheese**
- **2 tablespoons all-purpose flour**
- **3 eggs, beaten**
- **1 cup milk**
- **½ teaspoon salt Dash ground nutmeg**
- **1 (9-inch) pastry shell, baked**

Preheat oven to 400°F. Cook and stir onion in butter in small skillet until tender. Combine cooked onion, bacon, cheese and flour in small bowl. Combine eggs, milk, salt and nutmeg in large bowl. Stir in onion mixture. Pour into pastry shell. Bake 25 to 35 minutes or until center is set.

*Favorite recipe from **Wisconsin Milk Marketing Board***

Spinach-Stuffed Chicken Breasts

Sun-Dried Tomato and Pepper Stuffed Leg of Lamb with Garlic Chèvre Sauce

Makes 8 servings

- 1 (6- to 7-pound) leg of lamb, boned and butterflied
  Salt and black pepper
- 4½ ounces sun-dried tomatoes in oil, drained (about ¾ cup)
- 2 red or green bell peppers, roasted, peeled and seeded
- 1½ cups olive oil
- 2 tablespoons minced fresh rosemary
- 2 tablespoons minced fresh thyme
- 3 cloves garlic, minced
- 1 teaspoon TABASCO® pepper sauce
  Garlic Chèvre Sauce (recipe follows)

Set lamb, skin side down, on work surface. Pat dry. Sprinkle with salt and black pepper. Arrange tomatoes and bell peppers down center of lamb. Roll up lamb; secure with kitchen string. Set in roasting pan. Whisk oil, herbs, garlic and TABASCO sauce in small bowl. Pour over lamb, turning to coat. Cover and refrigerate 24 hours. Preheat oven to 450°F. Place uncovered lamb in oven and reduce temperature to 325°F. Cook about 2 hours or 20 minutes per pound. Let stand 15 minutes before slicing. Serve with Garlic Chèvre Sauce.

Sun-Dried Tomato and Pepper Stuffed Leg of Lamb

Garlic Chèvre Sauce

1 package (4 ounces) goat
   cheese
½ cup light cream
3 cloves garlic, minced
¼ teaspoon TABASCO®
   pepper sauce
1 sprig fresh rosemary

Combine goat cheese, cream, garlic
and TABASCO sauce in microwavable
dish; stir to combine. Microwave,
uncovered, at MEDIUM (50% power)
45 seconds. Let stand 5 minutes and
refrigerate. Garnish with rosemary
sprig.

Roast Turkey and Gravy

Makes 8 to 12 servings

1 PERDUE® fresh young
   turkey (12 to
   16 pounds)
2 tablespoons butter or
   margarine, melted
   Poultry seasoning to taste
   Salt and ground pepper to
   taste
1 onion, peeled (optional)
   Fresh fruit and herbs
   (optional)
4 tablespoons all-purpose
   flour
1 can (about 14 ounces)
   chicken broth
2 tablespoons sherry or
   port wine (optional)

Preheat oven to 325°F. Remove neck
and giblets from inside turkey;
discard fat from cavities. Rinse turkey
inside and out under cold running
water; pat dry. Brush turkey with
butter and season, inside and out,
with poultry seasoning, salt and
pepper. Place onion in large body
cavity; fold back wing tips. Check
that legs are secure in plastic holder
and Bird-Watcher thermometer is
flush against breast. Place turkey,
breast side up, in roasting pan.

Roast turkey, uncovered, 3 to 4 hours
or 15 to 20 minutes per pound until
thermometer pops up and juices run
clear when thigh is pierced, basting
occasionally. Remove and discard
thermometer and plastic leg holder.
Remove turkey to serving platter and
allow to stand in warm place 15 to
20 minutes before carving. Garnish
with fresh fruit and herbs.

To prepare gravy, pour pan juices
into heatproof bowl. With spoon,
skim off 4 tablespoons clear yellow
drippings from top of juices and
return to roasting pan. If using a
disposable pan, transfer to saucepan.
Skim off and discard remaining
yellow drippings and reserve
degreased pan juices.

Stir flour into drippings in pan and
place over medium heat. Cook 3 to
4 minutes until mixture is deep
golden brown, stirring constantly.
Add reserved pan juices, chicken
broth and sherry. Cook 3 to
4 minutes until gravy is smooth and
thickened, stirring constantly. Season
with salt and pepper.

Fettuccine Gorgonzola with Sun-Dried Tomatoes

Makes 4 servings

8 ounces uncooked spinach or tri-color fettuccine
1 cup low fat cottage cheese
½ cup plain nonfat yogurt
½ cup (2 ounces) crumbled Gorgonzola cheese
⅛ teaspoon ground white pepper
2 cups rehydrated sun-dried tomatoes* (4 ounces dry), cut into strips

*To rehydrate sun-dried tomatoes, pour 1 cup boiling water over tomatoes in small heatproof bowl. Let tomatoes soak 5 to 10 minutes or until soft. Drain.

Cook pasta according to package directions, omitting salt. Drain well. Cover to keep warm.

Combine cottage cheese and yogurt in food processor or blender; process until smooth. Heat cottage cheese mixture in small saucepan over low heat. Add Gorgonzola and white pepper; stir until cheese is melted.

Return pasta to saucepan; add tomatoes. Pour cheese mixture over pasta; mix well. Garnish as desired. Serve immediately.

German Beef Roulade

Makes 6 servings

1½ pounds flank steak
4 teaspoons GREY POUPON® Dijon Mustard
6 slices bacon, diced
¾ cup chopped onion
⅓ cup chopped dill pickle
¼ cup all-purpose flour
1 (13¾-fluid ounce) can COLLEGE INN® Beef Broth

With meat mallet or rolling pin, flatten meat to approximately a 10×8-inch rectangle. Spread mustard over meat.

In large skillet, over medium-high heat, cook bacon and onion until bacon is crisp; pour off fat, reserving ¼ cup. Spread bacon mixture over meat; sprinkle with pickle. Roll up meat from short end; secure with string.

In large skillet, over medium-high heat, brown beef roll in reserved fat; place in 13×9×2-inch baking dish. Stir flour into fat in skillet until smooth; gradually stir in beef broth. Cook and stir over medium heat until thickened. Pour sauce over beef roll. Cover; bake at 325°F for 1½ hours or until done. Let stand 10 minutes before slicing. Skim fat from sauce; strain and serve sauce with meat.

Fettuccine Gorgonzola with Sun-Dried Tomatoes

Herbed Scallops and Shrimp

Makes 4 servings

- ¼ **cup chopped fresh parsley**
- ¼ **cup lime juice**
- 2 **tablespoons chopped fresh mint**
- 2 **tablespoons chopped fresh rosemary**
- 1 **tablespoon honey**
- 1 **tablespoon olive oil**
- 2 **cloves garlic, minced**
- ¼ **teaspoon black pepper**
- ½ **pound jumbo shrimp, peeled and deveined**
- ½ **pound bay or halved sea scallops**

Preheat broiler. Combine parsley, lime juice, mint, rosemary, honey, oil, garlic and pepper in medium bowl; blend well. Add shrimp and scallops. Cover; refrigerate 1 hour.

Arrange shrimp and scallops on skewers. Place on broiler pan. Brush with marinade. Broil 5 to 6 minutes or until shrimp are opaque and scallops are lightly browned. Serve immediately with lime slices and fresh mint sprigs, if desired.

Herbed Scallops and Shrimp

Roast Turkey with Cornbread-Sausage Stuffing

Makes 12 servings

1 fresh or thawed frozen turkey (12 to 14 pounds); save giblets and neck for another use
Cornbread-Sausage Stuffing (recipe follows)
½ cup (1 stick) butter, melted
1 cup dry white wine or vermouth
3 tablespoons all-purpose flour
3 cups chicken broth
Salt and pepper

1. Preheat oven to 450°F. Rinse turkey; pat dry with paper towels. Prepare Cornbread Sausage Stuffing; stuff body and neck cavities loosely. Fold skin over openings and close with skewers. Tie legs together with cotton string. Tuck wings under turkey.

2. Place turkey on meat rack in shallow roasting pan. Insert meat thermometer in thickest part of thigh, not touching bone. Brush turkey evenly with one third of butter.

3. Place turkey in oven; *immediately reduce oven temperature to 325°F.* Roast 22 to 24 minutes per pound for a total roasting time of 4 to 5½ hours. Brush with butter after 1 hour and again 1½ hours later. Baste with pan juices after each hour. If turkey starts overbrowning, tent with foil. Turkey is done when internal temperature reaches 180°F and legs move easily in sockets.

4. Transfer turkey to cutting board. Pour off juices from pan; reserve. Pour wine into pan and place over burners. Cook over medium-high heat, scraping up browned bits and stirring constantly, 2 to 3 minutes or until mixture is reduced by half.

5. Transfer ⅓ cup fat from pan juices to large saucepan. (Discard any remaining fat.) Stir in flour; cook and stir over medium heat 1 minute. Slowly stir in chicken broth, wine mixture and defatted pan juice. Cook over medium heat 10 minutes, stirring occasionally. Season with salt and pepper.

Cornbread-Sausage Stuffing

8 ounces bulk pork sausage
½ cup butter or margarine
1 medium onion, chopped
½ cup celery, chopped
2 cloves garlic, minced
2 teaspoons dried sage
1 teaspoon poultry seasoning
1 package (16 ounces) prepared dry cornbread crumbs
¾ cup chicken broth

1. Brown sausage in large skillet over medium-high heat until no longer pink, stirring to separate meat. Drain on paper towels; set aside. Pour off grease from skillet.

2. Melt butter in same skillet over medium heat until foamy. Cook and stir onion, celery and garlic in butter until onion and celery are softened, about 10 minutes. Stir in sage and poultry seasoning; cook 1 minute more. Combine cornbread crumbs, sausage and onion mixture in large bowl. Drizzle broth over stuffing; toss lightly until evenly moistened.

Cookies & Confections

Pfeffernüsse

Makes about 5 dozen cookies

3½ cups all-purpose flour
2 teaspoons baking powder
1½ teaspoons ground cinnamon
1 teaspoon ground ginger
½ teaspoon baking soda
½ teaspoon salt
½ teaspoon ground cloves
½ teaspoon ground cardamom
¼ teaspoon freshly ground black pepper
1 cup butter, softened
1 cup granulated sugar
¼ cup dark molasses
1 egg
Powdered sugar

Grease cookie sheets. Place flour, baking powder, cinnamon, ginger, baking soda, salt, cloves, cardamom and pepper in large bowl; stir to combine. Beat butter and sugar in large bowl with electric mixer. Beat in molasses and egg. Gradually add flour mixture. Beat at low speed until dough forms. Wrap dough in plastic wrap; refrigerate until firm. Preheat oven to 350°F. Roll dough into 1-inch balls. Place 2 inches apart on prepared cookie sheets. Bake 12 to 14 minutes or until golden brown. Dust with sifted powdered sugar.

Smucker's® Crimson Ribbon Bars

Makes 20 bars

6 tablespoons butter or margarine, softened
½ cup firmly packed brown sugar
1 teaspoon vanilla
½ cup all-purpose flour
¼ teaspoon baking soda
1½ cups rolled oats
1 cup chopped walnuts
½ cup chopped figs
⅓ cup SMUCKER'S® Red Raspberry Preserves

Preheat oven to 375°F. Combine butter, brown sugar and vanilla; beat until well blended. Add flour and baking soda; mix well. Stir in oats and walnuts. Reserve ¾ cup oat mixture for topping. Press remaining oat mixture into 8-inch square baking pan coated with nonstick cooking spray. Combine figs and preserves; spread over oat mixture leaving ½-inch border. Sprinkle with reserved oat mixture; press lightly.

Bake 25 to 30 minutes or until golden brown. Cool in pan; cut into bars.

Smucker's® Crimson Ribbon Bars

Christmas Tree Cookies

Makes 1 1/2 to 3 dozen cookies

>   **1 package DUNCAN HINES®
>   Golden Sugar Cookie
>   Mix**
>   **2 eggs**
>   **1/3 cup CRISCO® Oil or
>   CRISCO® Puritan® Oil**
>   **Green food coloring**
>   **1/2 cup sliced natural
>   almonds**
>   **Pecan halves, cut in half**
>   **Red candied cherries, cut
>   in fourths**

1. Preheat oven to 375°F. Combine cookie mix, eggs, oil and 4 to 5 drops green food coloring in large bowl. Stir until thoroughly blended. Form dough into pea-size balls. Place 15 balls with sides touching in triangle shape on ungreased baking sheet. Repeat with remaining dough, placing cookies 2 inches apart.

2. Insert almond slices between balls to form branches. Place 1 pecan piece in bottom of each tree to form trunk. Place 1 cherry piece on top ball of each tree.

3. Bake 7 to 8 minutes or until cookies are set. Cool 1 minute on baking sheets. Remove to cooling racks. Cool completely. Store in airtight container.

Notes: For a delicious no-cholesterol variation, substitute 1 egg white for whole egg.

To keep dough from drying out, divide dough in half and wrap half in waxed paper or plastic wrap.

Tip: Cookies may be stored in airtight container in freezer for up to 6 months.

Almond Crescents

Makes about 5 dozen cookies

>   **1 cup butter or margarine,
>   softened**
>   **1 cup powdered sugar**
>   **2 egg yolks**
>   **2 1/2 cups all-purpose flour**
>   **1 1/2 teaspoons almond extract**
>   **Additional powdered
>   sugar**

Preheat oven to 375°F. Line cookie sheets with parchment paper or leave ungreased. Cream butter, sugar and egg yolks in large bowl. Beat in flour and almond extract until well mixed.

Shape dough into 1-inch balls. (If dough is too soft to handle, cover and refrigerate until firm.) Roll balls into 2-inch-long ropes, tapering both ends. Place 2 inches apart on cookie sheets. Curve ropes into crescent shapes; flatten slightly. Bake 8 to 10 minutes or until set, but not browned. Remove to wire rack. Cool completely. Dust with powdered sugar.

63

Welsh Tea Cakes

Makes about 3½ dozen tea cakes

- ¾ cup chopped dried mixed fruit or fruit bits or golden raisins
- 2 tablespoons brandy or cognac
- 2¼ cups all-purpose flour
- 2½ teaspoons cinnamon, divided
- 1 teaspoon baking powder
- ½ teaspoon baking soda
- ¼ teaspoon salt
- ¼ teaspoon ground cloves
- 1 cup butter, softened
- 1¼ cups sugar, divided
- 1 egg
- ⅓ cup sliced almonds (optional)

Preheat oven to 375°F.

Combine dried fruit and brandy in medium bowl; let sit at least 10 minutes to plump.

Place flour, 1½ teaspoons cinnamon, baking powder, baking soda, salt and cloves in medium bowl; stir to combine.

Beat butter and 1 cup sugar in large bowl with electric mixer at medium speed until light and fluffy, scraping down side of bowl once. Beat in egg. Gradually add flour mixture. Beat at low speed until well blended, scraping down side of bowl once. Stir in fruit mixture.

Combine remaining ¼ cup sugar and 1 teaspoon cinnamon in small bowl. Roll heaping teaspoonfuls of dough into 1-inch balls; roll balls in cinnamon sugar to coat. Place balls 2 inches apart on *ungreased* cookie sheets.

Press balls to ¼-inch thickness using bottom of glass dipped in granulated sugar. Press 3 almond slices horizontally into center of each cookie. (Almonds will spread evenly and flatten upon baking.)

Bake 10 to 12 minutes or until lightly browned. Remove tea cakes to wire racks; cool completely. Store tightly covered at room temperature or freeze up to 3 months.

Brickle Chips Pecan Dream Bars

Makes 2 dozen bars

- 1 cup butter
- 1 cup brown sugar
- 1 egg yolk
- 1 teaspoon vanilla
- 2 cups flour
- 1 package (6 ounces) BITS O'BRICKLE®, divided
- ½ cup finely chopped pecans

Preheat oven to 350°F.

Cream butter in large bowl with electric mixer at medium speed. Blend in sugar, egg yolk and vanilla. Stir in flour, ⅔ cup Bits O'Brickle® and pecans. Press into ungreased 15½ × 10½-inch jelly-roll pan.

Bake 18 to 20 minutes or until lightly browned. Remove from oven and immediately sprinkle remaining Bits O'Brickle® over top. Cool slightly; cut into squares.

Welsh Tea Cakes

Chocolate Pecan Pie Bars

Makes about 16 bars

- 1⅓ cups all-purpose flour
- 2 tablespoons *plus* ½ cup packed light brown sugar, divided
- ½ cup (1 stick) cold butter or margarine
- 2 eggs
- ½ cup light corn syrup
- ¼ cup HERSHEY®'S Cocoa
- 2 tablespoons butter or margarine, melted
- 1 teaspoon vanilla extract
- ⅛ teaspoon salt
- 1 cup coarsely chopped pecans

Heat oven to 350°F. In large bowl, stir together flour and 2 tablespoons brown sugar. With pastry blender, cut in ½ cup butter until mixture resembles coarse crumbs; press onto bottom and about 1 inch up sides of ungreased 9-inch square baking pan. Bake 10 to 12 minutes or until set. Remove from oven. With back of spoon, lightly press crust into corners and against sides of pan. In small bowl, lightly beat eggs, corn syrup, remaining ½ cup brown sugar, cocoa, 2 tablespoons butter, vanilla and salt until well blended. Stir in pecans. Pour mixture over warm crust. Continue baking 25 minutes or until pecan filling is set. Cool completely in pan on wire rack. Cut into bars.

Chocolate Amaretto Squares

Makes about 16 squares

- ½ cup (1 stick) butter (do not use margarine), melted
- 1 cup sugar
- 2 eggs
- ½ cup all-purpose flour
- ⅓ cup HERSHEY®'S Cocoa or HERSHEY®'S European Style Cocoa
- 2 tablespoons almond-flavored liqueur *or* ½ teaspoon almond extract
- 1¼ cups ground almonds
  Sliced almonds (optional)

Heat oven to 325°F. Grease 8-inch square baking pan. In large bowl, beat butter and sugar until creamy. Add eggs, flour and cocoa; beat well. Stir in almond liqueur and ground almonds. Pour batter into prepared pan. Bake 35 to 40 minutes or just until set. Cool completely in pan on wire rack. Cut into squares. Garnish with sliced almonds, if desired.

Clockwise from top right: Chunky Macadamia Bars (page 68), Chocolate Amaretto Squares and Chocolate Pecan Pie Bars

Chunky Macadamia Bars

Makes about 24 bars

- ¾ cup (1½ sticks) butter or margarine, softened
- 1 cup packed light brown sugar
- ½ cup granulated sugar
- 1 egg
- 1 teaspoon vanilla extract
- 2¼ cups all-purpose flour
- 1 teaspoon baking soda
- ¾ cup coarsely chopped macadamia nuts
- 1¾ cups (10-ounce package) HERSHEY®'S Semi-Sweet Chocolate Chunks, divided
- Quick Vanilla Glaze (recipe follows)

Heat oven to 375°F. In large mixer bowl, beat butter, brown sugar and granulated sugar until creamy. Add egg and vanilla; beat well. Add flour and baking soda; blend well. Stir in nuts and 1 cup chocolate chunks. Press dough onto bottom of ungreased 13×9×2-inch baking pan. Sprinkle with remaining ¾ cup chocolate chunks. Bake 22 to 25 minutes or until golden brown. Cool completely in pan on wire rack. Prepare Quick Vanilla Glaze; drizzle over top. Allow glaze to set. Cut into bars.

Quick Vanilla Glaze

- 1 cup powdered sugar
- 2 tablespoons milk
- ½ teaspoon vanilla extract

In small bowl, combine powdered sugar, milk and vanilla; stir until smooth and of desired consistency.

Cherry Chocolate No-Cook Fudge

Makes about 2 pounds

- 1 package (12 ounces) semisweet chocolate chips
- 1 can (14 ounces) sweetened condensed milk
- ¾ cup chopped pecans
- ½ cup chopped candied cherries
- 2 teaspoons vanilla
- Additional candied cherries for garnish (optional)

1. Butter 8-inch square pan; set aside.

2. Melt chocolate chips in heavy, small saucepan over very low heat, stirring constantly. Remove from heat.

3. Stir in condensed milk, pecans, chopped cherries and vanilla until combined. Spread in prepared pan. Score fudge into squares with knife. Refrigerate until firm.

4. Cut into squares. Decorate with additional candied cherries, if desired.

Chocolate Sugar Spritz

Makes 4 to 5 dozen cookies

2¼ cups all-purpose flour
¼ teaspoon salt
1 cup butter or margarine, softened
¾ cup granulated sugar
1 egg
1 teaspoon almond extract
2 squares (1 ounce each) unsweetened chocolate, melted
Assorted colored sprinkles for decorating (optional)

1. Preheat oven to 400°F.

2. Combine flour and salt in small bowl; stir to combine. Beat butter and sugar in large bowl with electric mixer at medium speed until light and fluffy. Beat in egg and almond extract. Beat in chocolate. Gradually add flour mixture with mixing spoon. (Dough will be stiff.)

3. Fit cookie press with desired plate (or change plates for different shapes after first batch). Fill press with dough; press dough 1 inch apart onto ungreased cookie sheets. Decorate with colored sprinkles, if desired.

4. Bake 7 minutes or until just set. Remove cookies to wire racks; cool completely.

Raspberry Coconut Layer Bars

Makes 24 (3×1½-inch) bar cookies

1⅔ cups graham cracker crumbs
½ cup butter, melted
2⅔ cups (7-ounce package) flaked coconut
1¼ cups (14-ounce can) CARNATION® Sweetened Condensed Milk
1 cup red raspberry jam or preserves
⅓ cup finely chopped walnuts, toasted
½ cup semisweet chocolate pieces, melted
¼ cup vanilla milk pieces, melted

In medium bowl, combine graham cracker crumbs and butter. Spread evenly over bottom of 13×9-inch baking pan, pressing firmly to make crust. Sprinkle coconut over crust. Pour sweetened condensed milk evenly over coconut. Bake in preheated 350°F oven 20 to 25 minutes or until lightly browned. Cool. Spread jam over milk layer. Chill 3 to 4 hours. Sprinkle with walnuts. Drizzle melted chocolates over top layer, making lacy effect. Cut into bars.

Double-Decker Fudge

Makes about 5 dozen pieces or about 2 pounds fudge

> 1 cup REESE'S® Peanut Butter Chips
> 1 cup HERSHEY®'S Semi-Sweet Chocolate Chips or HERSHEY®'S MINI CHIPS® Semi-Sweet Chocolate
> 2¼ cups sugar
> 1 jar (7 ounces) marshmallow creme
> ¾ cup evaporated milk
> ¼ cup (½ stick) butter or margarine
> 1 teaspoon vanilla extract

Line 8-inch square pan with foil, extending foil over edges of pan. In medium bowl, place peanut butter chips. In second medium bowl, place chocolate chips. In heavy 3-quart saucepan, combine sugar, marshmallow creme, evaporated milk and butter. Cook over medium heat, stirring constantly, until mixture comes to a boil; boil 5 minutes, stirring constantly. Remove from heat; stir in vanilla. Immediately stir half of the hot mixture (1½ cups) into peanut butter chips until chips are completely melted; quickly spread into prepared pan. Stir remaining hot mixture into chocolate chips until chips are completely melted. Quickly spread over top of peanut butter layer. Cool to room temperature; refrigerate until firm. Use foil to lift fudge out of pan; peel off foil. Cut into 1-inch squares. Store in tightly covered container at room temperature.

Christmas Spritz Cookies

Makes about 5 dozen cookies

> 2¼ cups all-purpose flour
> ¼ teaspoon salt
> 1¼ cups powdered sugar
> 1 cup butter, softened
> 1 large egg
> 1 teaspoon vanilla
> 1 teaspoon almond extract
> Assorted decorative sprinkles and candies (optional)

Preheat oven to 375°F. Place flour and salt in medium bowl; stir to combine. Beat powdered sugar and butter in large bowl with electric mixer until light and fluffy. Beat in egg, vanilla and almond extract. Gradually add flour mixture. Beat at low speed until well blended.

Divide dough in half. Fit cookie press with desired plate (or change plates for different shapes after first batch). Fill press with dough; press dough 1 inch apart onto ungreased cookie sheets. Decorate cookies with assorted decorative sprinkles, if desired.

Bake 10 to 12 minutes or until just set. Remove cookies to wire racks; cool completely. Store tightly covered at room temperature.

Note: Dough may be tinted by adding a few drops of food coloring.

Top to bottom:
Rich Cocoa Fudge (page 72)
and Double-Decker Fudge

Rich Cocoa Fudge

Makes about 3 dozen pieces or 1¾ pounds fudge

3 cups sugar
⅔ cup HERSHEY'S Cocoa or HERSHEY'S European Style Cocoa
⅛ teaspoon salt
1½ cups milk
¼ cup (½ stick) butter or margarine
1 teaspoon vanilla extract

Line 8- or 9-inch square pan with foil, extending foil over edges of pan. Butter foil. In heavy 4-quart saucepan, stir together sugar, cocoa and salt; stir in milk. Cook over medium heat, stirring constantly, until mixture comes to a full rolling boil. Boil, without stirring, until mixture reaches 234°F on candy thermometer or until syrup, when dropped into very cold water, forms a soft ball which flattens when removed from water. (Bulb of thermometer should not rest on bottom of saucepan.) Remove from heat. Add butter and vanilla. (Do not stir.) Cool at room temperature to 110°F (lukewarm). Beat with wooden spoon until fudge thickens and just begins to lose some of its gloss. Quickly spread into prepared pan; cool completely. Use foil to lift fudge out of pan; peel off foil. Cut into squares. Store in tightly covered container at room temperature.

Nutty Rich Cocoa Fudge:
Beat cooked fudge as directed. Immediately stir in 1 cup chopped almonds, pecans or walnuts; quickly spread into prepared pan.

Marshmallow-Nut Cocoa Fudge: Increase cocoa to ¾ cup. Cook fudge as directed. Add 1 cup marshmallow creme with butter and vanilla. (Do not stir.) Cool to 110°F (lukewarm). Beat 10 minutes; stir in 1 cup chopped nuts. Pour into prepared pan. (Fudge does not set until poured into pan.)

Note: For best results, do not double this recipe.

Butter Cookies

Makes about 2 dozen cookies

¾ cup butter or margarine, softened
¼ cup granulated sugar
¼ cup packed light brown sugar
1 egg yolk
1¾ cups all-purpose flour
¾ teaspoon baking powder
⅛ teaspoon salt
Frosting and colored sprinkles for decoration

1. Combine butter, granulated sugar, brown sugar and egg yolk in medium bowl. Add flour, baking powder and salt; mix well. Cover; refrigerate until firm, 4 hours or overnight.

2. Preheat oven to 350°F.

3. Roll dough on floured surface to ¼-inch thickness. Cut into desired shapes with cookie cutters. Place on ungreased cookie sheets.

4. Bake 8 to 10 minutes or until edges begin to brown. Remove to wire racks; cool completely.

5. Decorate with frosting and colored sprinkles as desired.

Snow Covered Almond Crescents

Snow Covered Almond Crescents

Makes about 3 dozen

    1 cup (2 sticks) margarine
        or butter, softened
    ¾ cup powdered sugar
    ½ teaspoon almond extract
        or 2 teaspoons vanilla
    1¾ cups all-purpose flour
    ¼ teaspoon salt (optional)
    1 cup QUAKER® Oats (quick
        or old fashioned,
        uncooked)
    ½ cup finely chopped
        almonds
        Powdered sugar

Preheat oven to 325°F. Beat margarine, sugar and almond extract until well blended. Add flour and salt; mix until well blended. Stir in oats and almonds. Using level measuring tablespoonfuls, shape dough into crescents. Bake on ungreased cookie sheet 14 to 17 minutes or until bottoms are light golden brown. Remove to wire rack. Sift additional powdered sugar generously over warm cookies. Cool completely. Store tightly covered.

Gingerbread People

Makes about 16 large cookies

**2¼ cups all-purpose flour
2 teaspoons ground
  cinnamon
2 teaspoons ground ginger
1 teaspoon baking powder
½ teaspoon salt
¼ teaspoon ground cloves
¼ teaspoon ground nutmeg
¾ cup butter, softened
½ cup packed light brown
  sugar
½ cup dark molasses
1 egg
  Red hot cinnamon candies
  Icing (recipe follows)
  Assorted other decors for
  decorating**

Place flour, cinnamon, ginger, baking powder, salt, cloves and nutmeg in large bowl; stir to combine.

Beat butter and brown sugar in large bowl with electric mixer at medium speed until light and fluffy, scraping down side of bowl once. Beat in molasses and egg. Gradually add flour mixture. Beat at low speed until well blended, scraping down side of bowl once.

Form dough into 3 discs. Wrap dough in plastic wrap; refrigerate 1 hour or until firm.

Preheat oven to 350°F. Working with 1 disc at a time, unwrap dough and place on lightly floured surface. Roll out dough with lightly floured rolling pin to ³⁄₁₆-inch thickness.

Cut out gingerbread people with floured 5-inch cookie cutters.

Place cutouts on *ungreased* cookie sheets. If desired, press red hot cinnamon candies into dough for eyes or coat buttons.

Gently press dough trimmings together; reroll and cut out more cookies.

Bake about 12 minutes or until edges are golden brown. Let cookies stand on cookie sheets 1 minute. Remove cookies with spatula to wire racks; cool completely.

Prepare Icing. If desired, Icing may be divided into small bowls and tinted with food coloring to use for decorative piping.

Spoon Icing into small resealable plastic freezer bag. Cut off tiny corner of one end of bag. Pipe Icing decoratively onto cooled cookies; press red hots or candies into Icing. Let stand at room temperature 20 minutes or until set. Store tightly covered at room temperature or freeze up to 3 months.

Icing

**1½ cups powdered sugar
2 tablespoons milk plus
  additional if needed
½ teaspoon vanilla**

Place all ingredients in medium bowl; stir with spoon until thick, but spreadable. (If Icing is too thick, stir in 1 teaspoon additional milk.)

Gingerbread People

Desserts

Early American Pumpkin Pie

Makes 6 to 8 servings

1½ cups cooked pumpkin, canned or fresh
  1 cup whole or 2% milk
  2 eggs, beaten
  1 cup sugar
  ½ teaspoon ground cinnamon
  ¼ teaspoon salt
  ¼ teaspoon ground ginger
  ¼ teaspoon ground nutmeg
  1 tablespoon butter or margarine, melted
  1 (9-inch) unbaked pie shell
    Sweetened whipped cream or whipped topping
       (optional)
    Fresh currants (optional)

Preheat oven to 425°F. Combine all ingredients except pie shell, cream and currants in large bowl; blend well. Pour into pie shell. Bake 45 to 50 minutes or until knife inserted into filling comes out clean. Cool completely. Serve with whipped cream and garnish with currants, if desired. Refrigerate leftovers.

*Favorite recipe from **Bob Evans Farms**®*

Eggnog Cheesecake

Eggnog Cheesecake

Makes 12 servings

CRUST
>   2 cups vanilla wafer cookie
>   crumbs
>   6 tablespoons margarine,
>   melted
>   ½ teaspoon ground nutmeg

FILLING
>   4 packages (8 ounces each)
>   PHILADELPHIA
>   BRAND® Cream Cheese,
>   softened
>   1 cup sugar
>   3 tablespoons all-purpose
>   flour
>   3 tablespoons rum
>   1 teaspoon vanilla
>   2 eggs
>   1 cup whipping cream
>   4 egg yolks

• Heat oven to 325°F.

• To prepare Crust, mix together crumbs, spread and nutmeg; press onto bottom and 1½ inches up side of 9-inch springform pan. Bake 10 minutes.

• To prepare Filling, beat cream cheese, sugar, flour, rum and vanilla with electric mixer at medium speed until well blended. Add eggs, 1 at a time, mixing at low speed after each addition, just until blended. Blend in whipping cream and egg yolks; pour into crust.

• Bake 1 hour and 10 minutes to 1 hour and 15 minutes or until center is almost set. Run knife or metal spatula around rim of pan to loosen cake; cool before removing rim of pan. Refrigerate 4 hours or overnight. Garnish with thawed COOL WHIP® Whipped Topping and ground nutmeg.

Prep Time: 25 minutes plus refrigerating
Cook Time: 1 hour 15 minutes

78

Mocha Almond Roll

Makes 8 to 10 servings

3¼ **cups cake flour**
1 **teaspoon baking powder**
¼ **teaspoon salt**
3 **eggs**
1 **cup granulated sugar**
⅓ **cup water**
1½ **teaspoons vanilla extract,
    divided**
½ **teaspoon almond extract
    Powdered sugar**
1 **cup BLUE DIAMOND®
    Blanched Almond Paste**
2¾ **cups heavy cream, divided**
6 **ounces semisweet
    chocolate chips**
3¼ **cups powdered sugar**
3 **tablespoons coffee-
    flavored liqueur
    Chocolate curls (see Note)**

Line a 15½×10×½-inch jelly-roll pan with parchment or waxed paper; thoroughly grease with shortening.

Combine flour, baking powder and salt; reserve. Beat eggs at high speed until foamy, about 3 to 5 minutes. Gradually beat in granulated sugar. On low speed, beat in water, ½ teaspoon vanilla and almond extract. Gradually beat in flour mixture until smooth. Pour evenly into pan.

Bake in 375°F oven 12 to 15 minutes or until wooden toothpick inserted into center comes out clean. Meanwhile, sift powdered sugar onto a clean dishtowel until evenly coated.

When cake is done, immediately turn out from pan onto prepared towel. Peel off parchment. Roll up cake and towel together, starting from narrow end; cool thoroughly on wire rack.

Using rolling pin, spread almond paste between 2 sheets of waxed paper into 15×10-inch rectangle; reserve.

Heat ¾ cup cream and chocolate chips, whisking until smooth. Remove chocolate mixture from heat and stir occasionally until thickened; reserve. Whip remaining 2 cups cream, 3¼ cups powdered sugar, liqueur and remaining 1 teaspoon vanilla until soft peaks form. Whisk in ⅓ cup chocolate mixture; beat until stiff peaks form.

Unroll cooled cake. Spread remaining chocolate mixture on cake. Remove waxed paper from one side of almond paste rectangle; turn rectangle, almond paste side down, onto top of chocolate mixture on cake. Peel off remaining waxed paper.

Spread 1¼ cups whipped cream mixture over almond paste, leaving 1-inch border at one short edge. Carefully roll up cake from opposite end. Transfer to platter, placing seam side down. Frost cake with remaining whipped cream mixture. Garnish with chocolate curls. Refrigerate until ready to serve.

Note: To make chocolate curls, hold block of chocolate over plate. Draw blade of vegetable peeler or knife along narrow edge of chocolate block. Chill curls immediately. Place on cake using tip of knife or toothpick.

Creamy Chocolate Dipped Strawberries

Makes about 3 dozen dipped berries

1 cup HERSHEY'S Semi-Sweet Chocolate Chips
½ cup HERSHEY'S Vanilla Milk Chips
1 tablespoon shortening (do not use butter, margarine or oil)
Fresh strawberries, rinsed and patted dry (about 2 pints)

Line tray with waxed paper. In medium microwave-safe bowl, place chocolate chips, vanilla milk chips and shortening. Microwave at HIGH (100%) 1 minute; stir. If necessary, microwave at HIGH an additional 15 seconds at a time, stirring after each heating, just until chips are melted when stirred. Holding top, dip bottom two-thirds of each strawberry into melted mixture; shake gently to remove excess. Place on prepared tray. Refrigerate about 1 hour or until coating is firm. Cover; refrigerate leftover dipped berries. For best results, use within 24 hours.

Linzertorte

Makes 12 servings

1¼ cups all-purpose flour
1 cup QUAKER® Oats (quick or old fashioned, uncooked)
1 cup plus 1 tablespoon powdered sugar, divided
¼ cup finely chopped almonds
1 tablespoon grated lemon peel
⅔ cup (1⅓ sticks) margarine
2 tablespoons water
1 jar (10 ounces) no-added-sugar raspberry fruit spread

Preheat oven to 350°F. Combine flour, oats, 1 cup powdered sugar, almonds and lemon peel. Cut in margarine until crumbly. Stir in water until dough is moistened. Reserve 1 cup; set aside. Press remaining dough onto bottom and 1 inch up side of ungreased 9-inch springform pan or 9-inch square baking pan. Bake 20 minutes. Spread crust with fruit spread. Roll reserved dough into ¼-inch-thick ropes; decorate top with crisscrossing dough. Bake 30 to 35 minutes or until light golden brown. Cool. Sprinkle with remaining 1 tablespoon powdered sugar before serving.

Orange Pumpkin Tart

Makes 12 servings

- **1½ cups all-purpose flour**
- **1 cup QUAKER® Oats (quick or old fashioned, uncooked), divided**
- **1 cup plus 2 tablespoons sugar, divided**
- **¾ cup (1½ sticks) margarine**
- **2 tablespoons water**
- **1 can (16 ounces) pumpkin (1¾ cups)**
- **1 egg white**
- **1 teaspoon pumpkin pie spice**
- **½ cup powdered sugar**
- **2 teaspoons orange juice**
- **½ teaspoon grated orange peel**

Preheat oven to 400°F. Combine flour, ¾ cup oats and ½ cup sugar; cut in margarine until crumbly. Reserve ¾ cup oat mixture. Mix remaining oat mixture with water until dough is moistened. Divide into 2 parts; press each onto cookie sheet to form a 12×5-inch tart. Combine pumpkin, egg white, ½ cup sugar and pumpkin pie spice. Spread over tarts. Top with combined remaining ¼ cup oats, remaining 2 tablespoons sugar and reserved oat mixture. Bake 25 minutes or until golden. Cool. Drizzle with combined remaining ingredients. Refrigerate leftovers.

Orange Pumpkin Tart

Rich Chocolate Glazed Cream Puffs

Makes 12 servings

1 cup water
½ cup (1 stick) butter or
   margarine
¼ teaspoon salt
1 cup all-purpose flour
4 eggs
   Chocolate Cream Filling
   (recipe follows)
   Rich Chocolate Glaze
   (recipe follows)
   Fresh strawberries
   (optional)

Heat oven to 400°F. Lightly grease cookie sheet. In medium saucepan, heat water, butter and salt to full rolling boil; reduce heat to low. Add flour all at once; beat with spoon until mixture forms ball. Remove from heat. Add eggs, one at a time, beating well after each addition until mixture is smooth. Drop by spoonfuls into 12 balls onto prepared cookie sheet. Bake 35 to 40 minutes or until golden brown. While puff is warm, horizontally slice off small portion of top; reserve top. Remove any soft dough from inside of puff; cool puffs on wire rack. Prepare Chocolate Cream Filling and Rich Chocolate Glaze. Fill puffs with filling; replace tops. Drizzle with prepared glaze. Garnish with fresh strawberries, if desired.

Chocolate Cream Filling

½ cup sugar
⅓ cup all-purpose flour
½ teaspoon salt
2½ cups milk
2 egg yolks, slightly beaten
1 cup HERSHEY'S Semi-
   Sweet Chocolate Chips
1 tablespoon butter or
   margarine
2 teaspoons vanilla extract

In medium saucepan, stir together sugar, flour and salt; gradually add milk. Cook over medium heat, stirring constantly, until mixture comes to a boil; boil 2 minutes, stirring constantly. Gradually stir half of mixture into egg yolks; return to saucepan. Cook, stirring constantly, 1 minute. Remove from heat; stir in chocolate chips, butter and vanilla until mixture is smooth. Pour into bowl; press plastic wrap directly onto surface. Cool; refrigerate 1 to 2 hours or until cold.

Rich Chocolate Glaze

½ cup HERSHEY'S Semi-
   Sweet Chocolate Chips
1 tablespoon shortening (do
   not use butter,
   margarine or oil)

In small microwave-safe bowl, place chocolate chips and shortening. Microwave at HIGH (100%) 1 minute; stir. If necessary, microwave at HIGH an additional 15 seconds at a time, stirring after each heating, just until chips are melted.

Top to bottom: Creamy Chocolate Dipped Strawberries (page 80) and Rich Chocolate Glazed Cream Puffs

Minted Pears with Gorgonzola

Makes 4 servings

**4 whole firm pears with
stems, peeled
2 cups Concord grape juice
1 tablespoon honey
1 tablespoon finely chopped
fresh mint
1 cinnamon stick
1/4 teaspoon ground nutmeg
1/4 cup Gorgonzola cheese,
crumbled**

Place pears in medium saucepan.
Add grape juice, honey, mint,
cinnamon stick and nutmeg. Bring to
a boil over high heat. Cover and
simmer 15 to 20 minutes, turning
pears once to absorb juices evenly.
Cook until pears can be easily
pierced with fork. Remove from heat;
cool. Remove pears with slotted
spoon; set aside. Discard cinnamon
stick.

Bring juice mixture to a boil; simmer
20 minutes. Pour over pears. Sprinkle
Gorgonzola around pears.

Minted Pears with Gorgonzola

White Chocolate Cheesecake

Makes 12 servings

CRUST
- ½ **cup (1 stick) butter**
- ¼ **cup sugar**
- ½ **teaspoon vanilla**
- 1 **cup all-purpose flour**

FILLING
- 4 **packages (8 ounces each) PHILADELPHIA BRAND® Cream Cheese, softened**
- ½ **cup sugar**
- 1 **teaspoon vanilla**
- 4 **eggs**
- 12 **ounces white chocolate, melted, slightly cooled**

- Heat oven to 325°F.

- For Crust, cream butter, sugar and vanilla in small bowl with electric mixer at medium speed until light and fluffy. Gradually add flour, mixing at low speed until blended. Press onto bottom of 9-inch springform pan; prick with fork.

- Bake 25 minutes or until edges are light golden brown.

- For Filling, beat cream cheese, sugar and vanilla with electric mixer at medium speed until well blended. Add eggs, 1 at a time, mixing at low speed after each addition, just until blended. Blend in melted chocolate; pour over crust.

- Bake 55 to 60 minutes or until center is almost set. Run knife or metal spatula around rim of pan to loosen cake; cool before removing rim of pan. Refrigerate 4 hours or overnight. Garnish with chocolate curls; sprinkle with powdered sugar.

Macadamia Nut: Stir in 1 jar (3½ ounces) macadamia nuts, chopped (about ¾ cup).

Prep Time: 25 minutes plus refrigerating
Cook Time: 1 hour 25 minutes

Holiday Eggnog Cream

Makes 3½ cups

- 2 **tablespoons cornstarch**
- 2 **tablespoons sugar**
- ½ **teaspoon ground nutmeg**
- 1½ **cups dairy eggnog**
- 2 **teaspoons rum extract**
- ½ **cup dairy sour cream**
- 1 **cup whipping cream, whipped**

Combine cornstarch, sugar and nutmeg in large saucepan; gradually add eggnog. Stir in extract. Bring to boil over medium heat, stirring constantly. Boil 1 minute or until thickened, stirring constantly. Stir in sour cream; remove from heat. Cool. Fold in whipped cream; refrigerate several hours. Serve as a topping for pound cake slices, pumpkin pie or as a sauce or dip for fresh fruit or cookies.

Favorite recipe from ***Wisconsin Milk Marketing Board***

85

Apple-Cranberry Crisp

Makes 9 servings

- 1½ cups QUAKER® Oats (quick or old fashioned, uncooked)
- ½ cup firmly packed brown sugar
- ⅓ cup all-purpose flour
- ½ teaspoon ground cinnamon
- ⅓ cup vegetable shortening, melted
- 1 tablespoon water
- 1 can (16 ounces) whole berry cranberry sauce
- 2 tablespoons cornstarch
- 5 cups peeled and thinly sliced apples (about 5 medium)

Preheat oven to 375°F. For topping, combine oats, brown sugar, flour and cinnamon; mix well. Stir in melted shortening and water; mix until crumbly. Set aside.

For filling, combine cranberry sauce and cornstarch in large saucepan; mix well. Heat over medium-heat, stirring occasionally, 2 minutes or until sauce bubbles. Add apples, tossing to coat. Spread into 8-inch baking dish. Crumble topping over fruit. Bake 25 to 35 minutes or until apples are tender. Serve warm with whipped cream or ice cream, if desired.

Apple-Cranberry Crisp

Chocolate Whipped Cream Torte

Makes 8 servings

> 6 eggs, separated
> ¾ cup granulated sugar, divided
> ⅔ cup butter, softened
> 1⅓ cups finely chopped walnuts
> 4 squares (4 ounces) semisweet chocolate, melted and cooled
> 2 tablespoons flour
> 1 teaspoon vanilla
> ½ cup raspberry preserves, divided
> Vanilla Whipped Cream (recipe follows)
> Chocolate Whipped Cream (recipe follows)
> Chocolate curls, raspberries and walnut pieces for garnish

Preheat oven to 325°F. Butter 15×10×1-inch jelly-roll pan. Line bottom with waxed paper. Butter waxed paper; set aside.

In large bowl of electric mixer, beat egg whites until soft peaks form. Beat in ½ cup sugar, 2 tablespoons at a time, until stiff peaks form; set aside. In another large bowl, using electric mixer, beat egg yolks, remaining ¼ cup sugar, butter, walnuts, chocolate, flour and vanilla; beat until light and fluffy, about 4 minutes. Using rubber spatula, gently fold in egg white mixture just until blended; pour into prepared pan.

Bake until toothpick inserted into center comes out clean, about 15 minutes. Cool on wire rack 10 minutes. Remove cake from pan; place on large wire rack or baking sheet. Remove waxed paper; cool completely.

To assemble, trim edges from cake; cut cake crosswise into 3 equal rectangles. Place 1 layer on cake plate; spread with half of raspberry preserves. Set aside small amount of Vanilla Whipped Cream for garnish. Spread cake with half remaining Vanilla Whipped Cream. Top with second cake layer; repeat with remaining jam and Vanilla Whipped Cream. Top with third cake layer; frost with Chocolate Whipped Cream. Garnish with remaining Vanilla Whipped Cream, chocolate curls, raspberries and walnut pieces, if desired. Cake may be made 1 to 2 days ahead; cover and refrigerate. Fill and frost day of serving.

Vanilla Whipped Cream

> 1 cup whipping cream
> ¼ cup powdered sugar
> 1 teaspoon vanilla extract

In deep bowl, using electric mixer, beat cream, sugar and vanilla until soft peaks form.

Chocolate Whipped Cream

> 1 cup whipping cream
> ½ cup powdered sugar
> ¼ cup unsweetened cocoa

In deep bowl, using electric mixer, beat cream, sugar and cocoa until soft peaks form.

*Favorite recipe from **National Dairy Board***

Pumpkin Pecan Pie

Makes 8 servings

- 3 eggs, divided
- 1 cup canned solid pack pumpkin
- 1 cup sugar, divided
- 1/2 teaspoon cinnamon
- 1/4 teaspoon ground ginger
- 1/8 teaspoon ground cloves
- 1 (9-inch) frozen deep dish pie crust*
- 2/3 cup KARO® Light or Dark Corn Syrup
- 2 tablespoons MAZOLA® margarine or butter, melted
- 1 teaspoon vanilla
- 1 cup coarsely chopped pecans or walnuts

To use prepared frozen pie crust: Do not thaw. Preheat oven and a cookie sheet. Pour filling into frozen crust. Bake on cookie sheet.

Preheat oven to 350°F. In small bowl, combine 1 egg, pumpkin, 1/3 cup sugar, cinnamon, ginger and cloves. Spread evenly in bottom of pie crust. In medium bowl, beat remaining 2 eggs slightly. Stir in corn syrup, remaining 2/3 cup sugar, margarine and vanilla until blended. Stir in pecans; carefully spoon over pumpkin mixture.

Bake 50 to 60 minutes or until filling is set around edge. Cool completely on wire rack.

Prep Time: 15 minutes
Bake Time: 50 minutes, plus cooling

PHILLY® Sparkling Strawberry Mold

Makes 6 to 8 servings

- 1½ cups boiling water
- 2 packages (4-serving size each) JELL-O® Brand Strawberry Flavor Gelatin
- 3/4 cup ginger ale
- 1 package (8 ounces) PHILADELPHIA BRAND® Cream Cheese, softened
- 1 package (10 ounces) frozen strawberries

• Stir boiling water into gelatin in medium bowl 2 minutes or until completely dissolved. Stir in ginger ale.

• Beat cream cheese with electric mixer at medium speed until smooth. Gradually add gelatin mixture in very small amounts, mixing at medium speed until well blended. Stir in strawberries.

• Pour into 1½-quart mold. Refrigerate until firm. Unmold onto serving plate. Garnish with COOL WHIP® Whipped Topping and strawberries.

Note: May also use PHILADELPHIA BRAND® Neufchâtel Cheese, 1/3 Less Fat Than Cream Cheese or PHILADELPHIA BRAND FREE® Fat Free Cream Cheese.

Prep Time: 20 minutes plus refrigerating

Pumpkin Pecan Pie

Chocolate Steamed Pudding

Makes 8 servings

1½ (1-ounce) squares
    unsweetened chocolate
1 tablespoon butter
1 cup sugar
2 eggs
½ teaspoon vanilla
¾ cup hot coffee
1½ cups all-purpose flour
1½ teaspoons baking powder
¼ teaspoon salt
    Ellie's Mom's Sauce
    (recipe follows)

Preheat oven to 350°F. Melt chocolate with butter in small saucepan over very low heat. Remove from heat and cool. Combine sugar, eggs and vanilla in large bowl; beat well. Blend in coffee. Sift together dry ingredients in separate large bowl. Add to sugar mixture; mix well. Blend chocolate mixture into sugar mixture. Divide batter evenly among 8 buttered (6-ounce) custard cups. Cover each tightly with aluminum foil. Place cups in pan with at least 1-inch sides; fill with ½ inch very hot water. Cover pan tightly with aluminum foil. Bake 45 minutes. Cool; unmold. Serve warm with Ellie's Mom's Sauce.

Ellie's Mom's Sauce

1¼ cups sifted powdered
    sugar
5 tablespoons butter,
    melted
1 egg
¾ teaspoon vanilla
⅛ teaspoon salt
½ cup whipping cream

Combine all ingredients except whipping cream in small bowl; mix well. Beat cream in medium bowl until thickened. Fold sugar mixture into whipped cream until combined.

*Favorite recipe from **Wisconsin Milk Marketing Board***

Marble Cheesecake

Makes 10 to 12 servings

HERSHEY®'S Chocolate
    Crumb Crust (recipe
    follows)
3 packages (8 ounces each)
    cream cheese, softened
1 cup sugar, divided
½ cup dairy sour cream
2½ teaspoons vanilla extract,
    divided
3 tablespoons all-purpose
    flour
3 eggs
¼ cup HERSHEY®'S Cocoa
1 tablespoon vegetable oil

Prepare HERSHEY®'S Chocolate Crumb Crust. Heat oven to 450°F. In large mixer bowl on medium speed of electric mixer, beat cream cheese, ¾ cup sugar, sour cream and

2 teaspoons vanilla until smooth. Gradually add flour, beating well. Add eggs, one at a time, beating well after each addition.

In medium bowl, stir together cocoa and remaining ¼ cup sugar. Add oil, remaining ½ teaspoon vanilla and 1½ cups cream cheese mixture; blend well. Spoon plain and chocolate batters alternately into prepared crust, ending with spoonfuls of chocolate batter; gently swirl with knife for marbled effect. Bake 10 minutes. *Without opening oven door, reduce temperature to 250°F;* continue baking 30 minutes. Turn off oven; without opening door, leave cheesecake in oven 30 minutes. Remove from oven to wire rack. With knife, immediately loosen cheesecake from side of pan; cool completely. Refrigerate several hours or overnight; remove side of pan. Cover; refrigerate leftover cheesecake.

HERSHEY'S Chocolate Crumb Crust

**1¼ cups vanilla wafer crumbs
(about 40 wafers)
⅓ cup powdered sugar
⅓ cup HERSHEY'S Cocoa
¼ cup (½ stick) butter or
margarine, melted**

Heat oven to 350°F. In medium bowl, stir together crumbs, powdered sugar and cocoa; blend in butter. Press mixture onto bottom and ½ inch up side of 9-inch springform pan. Bake 8 minutes; cool completely.

Marble Cheesecake

Acknowledgments

**The publisher would like to thank the companies and
organizations listed below for the use of their recipes
and photographs in this publication.**

Best Foods, a Division of CPC International Inc.

Blue Diamond Growers

Bob Evans Farms®

Dole Food Company, Inc.

Golden Grain/Mission Pasta

Hershey Foods Corporation

Kraft Foods, Inc.

Lawry's® Foods, Inc.

Leaf®, Inc.

McIlhenny Company

Minnesota Cultivated Wild Rice Council

Nabisco, Inc.

National Dairy Board

National Fisheries Institute

National Cattlemen's Beef Association

Nestlé Food Company

Norseland, Inc.

Perdue® Farms

The Procter & Gamble Company

The Quaker Oats Company

RED STAR® Yeast & Products, A Division

of Universal Foods Corporation

The J.M. Smucker Company

The Sugar Association, Inc.

Wisconsin Milk Marketing Board

Index

INDEX